# A Country Christmas

TIME-LIFE BOOKS

Alexandria, Virginia

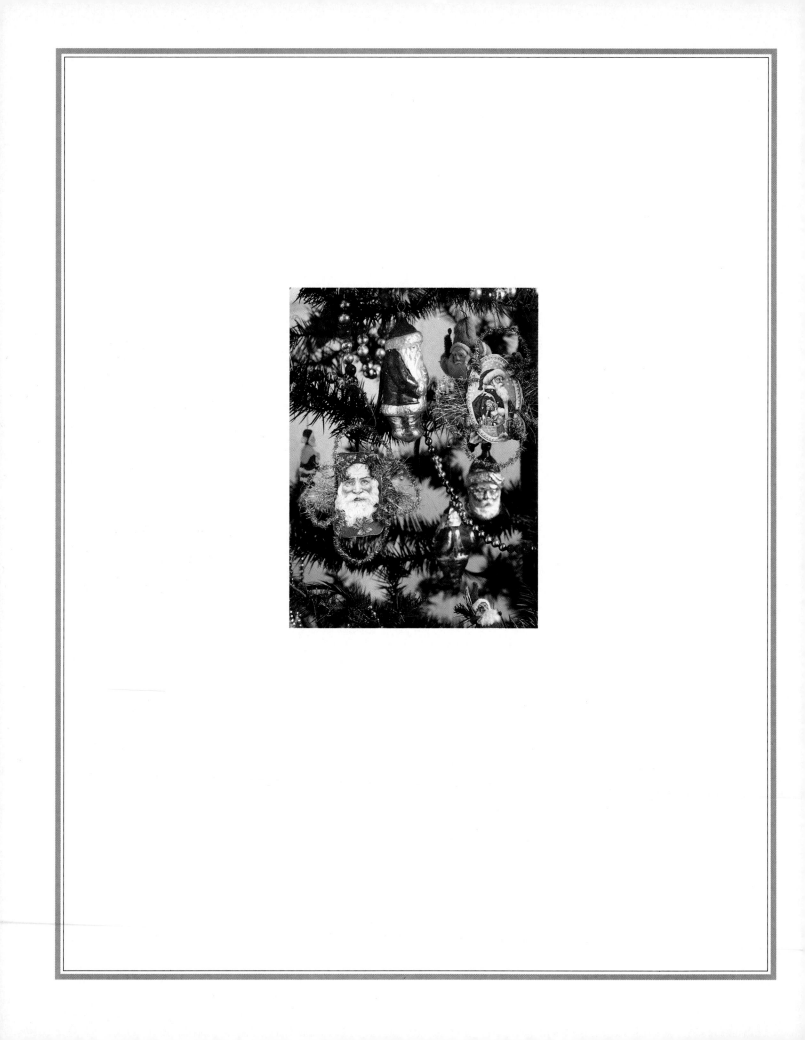

# A Country Christmas

*a celebration of
the holiday season*

A REBUS BOOK

# C O N T E N T S

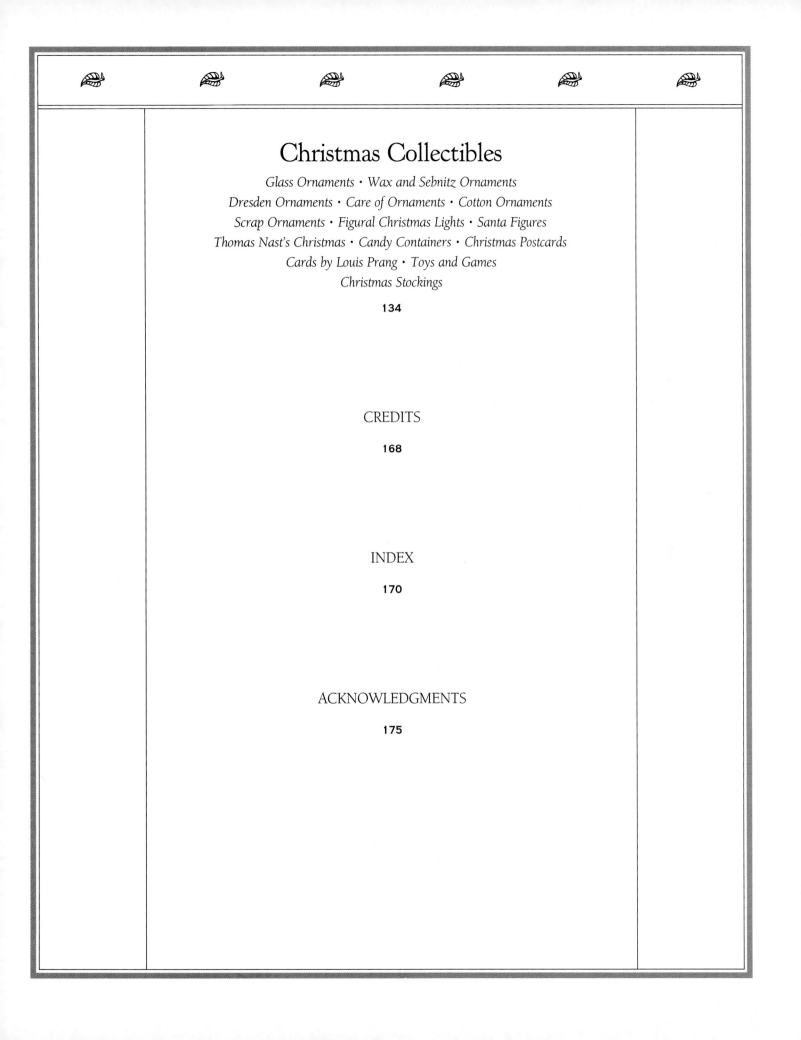

## Christmas Collectibles

*Glass Ornaments · Wax and Sebnitz Ornaments*
*Dresden Ornaments · Care of Ornaments · Cotton Ornaments*
*Scrap Ornaments · Figural Christmas Lights · Santa Figures*
*Thomas Nast's Christmas · Candy Containers · Christmas Postcards*
*Cards by Louis Prang · Toys and Games*
*Christmas Stockings*

No holiday holds a stronger place in the American imagination than Christmas. In part, the magic lies in the anticipation, as we await the arrival of family members, prepare for holiday parties, or watch for the surprise on a friend's face as a carefully chosen gift is opened. There is also joy to be found in the annual ritual of decorating, which might involve setting out a collection of antique ornaments, trimming a wreath, or stringing garlands. And of course there is the tree, often the subject of friendly debate each year. Should it be a bushy Scotch pine, an elegant blue spruce, or perhaps a balsam, favored for its evocative scent? Whatever the type of tree and greens you choose, a country Christmas is unthinkable without them.

Perhaps the reason that familiar traditions like these form such a firm foundation for Christmas celebrations is that they are deeply rooted in history. In most ancient, pre-Christian cultures throughout Europe and Britain, the winter solstice and the beginning of a new solar year were celebrated with festivals and feasting at the end of December. Considered sacred, evergreens, which symbolized everlasting life, played an important ritualistic role in these festivities. Some greens, especially those that bore fruit in winter, were believed to have magical properties. Holly, for instance, was used for divining the future, while mistletoe, called the "all-healer," was thought to cure infertility in animals.

The first mention of a Nativity feast on December 25 dates from the middle of the 4th century in Rome. Because no one knows which month or even what time of year the birth of Christ actually took place, it is thought that early Christians chose a December date that coincided with the pagan rituals in order to overshadow these "heathen" celebrations with their own religious holiday. Initially, Christians tried to prohibit the use of greenery at Nativity feasts, but it was gradually permitted in homes and then in some churches. The association of trees with Christmas may have begun with the medieval "paradise tree," decorated with apples, which was central to the Christian Adam and Eve plays that were performed in December. The first record of decorated fir trees being set up in parlors at Christmas, dated 1605, describes a tree similar to the paradise tree, in the Alsatian town of Strasbourg.

As time went on, some Christians accepted the formalities of Christmas more readily than others. The Puritans and other reformers who settled in New England considered Christmas a pagan holiday, and had no use for the feasting and frivolity that went along with it. (In 1659, a law was passed in Connecticut forbidding the celebration of Christmas and the baking of mince pies.) On the other hand, the Dutch in New York, the Germans and Moravians in Pennsylvania and North Carolina, and the English in Virginia observed the holiday season by attending church and indulging in general merrymaking. It was not until after the Revolutionary period, however, that Christmas observances became more widespread. Decorated trees were introduced in Pennsylvania-German communities in the early 1800s, and by 1856 a tree was set up in the White House. Complete with greenery, ornaments, and feasting, Christmas was well on its way to becoming America's favorite holiday.

# Decking the Halls

*some of the many ways
to decorate for a country
Christmas*

Celebrating the holidays often begins with decorating the house. Before the first gift is wrapped or cookie baked, many families are already busy setting up a tree and unpacking ornaments. Some people derive so much pleasure from the season that they start decking the halls at Thanksgiving, and for those who like to make their own trimmings, preparations can commence even earlier in the year. Only after New Year's Day is the holiday finery reluctantly packed away.

As the houses in this chapter reveal, the essence of a country Christmas is found in friendly, homespun celebrations. Often, it is the simplest decorations that are the most effective: a garland of fresh pine boughs caught with ribbon bows, dried flowers used as tree ornaments, a few pinecones and apples clustered on a mantelpiece, a wreath on a door, a candle in a window. Antique ornaments and feather trees, handcrafted Santas, Belsnickels, Nativity animals, and vintage toys also find a welcome place among the trimmings—expressions, all, of holiday good will.

*Toys and a feather tree are part of an old-fashioned holiday still life.*

# A
# Festive
# Farmhouse

Familiar traditions make Christmas cele-brations memorable for the owners of this 19th-century residence, originally part of a large Wisconsin farmstead. Every year the family host an open house, a Christmas Eve fondue party, and a treasure hunt for gifts.

An appreciation for tradition also influences the homeowners' choice of Christmas trim-mings; long-time antiques collectors who par-ticularly enjoy toys and folk art with an animal theme, they base their holiday decor on their favorite pieces. They try to include their collect-

ibles in Christmas arrangements, and might add a jaunty bow to a carved piece or top a painting with a bit of greenery. Their holiday decorating extends not only throughout the house, but also to the bed-and-breakfast cottage they have remodeled from an old smokehouse on the farm.

Appropriately, the tree is set up in the family room, the busiest room in the house, where much of the season's entertaining takes place. Here, the seven-foot balsam fir sparkles with tiny white lights and antique trimmings such as German glass kugels, clip-on candleholders,

*Continued*

*The Wisconsin farmhouse at left was built in 1844 and still has its original clapboards and small "eyebrow" windows. At Christmas, the exterior is simply decorated with a wreath on the front door; a single candle glows in each window.*

*The mid-19th-century toy rocking horse atop the old cupboard in the family room above wears a bow-bedecked wreath around its neck. A red-and-green Double Irish Chain quilt is hung behind at Christmas time.*

wax angels, bead chains, cotton-batting ornaments, and a spun-glass angel at the top. Homemade popcorn garlands and ornaments made by the family's two children add a personal touch. Near the tree, flowering poinsettias—one placed in an old painted bucket, others in a buttocks basket—bring additional Christmas color to the room.

To take advantage of the large windows in the family room, ropes of greenery caught with red-ribbon bows are looped across the panes. On the windowsills, farm animals—pull-toy cows and horses and an old tin cow weathervane—are set out to "pasture." *Continued*

*Red tree ornaments, poinsettias, and bows bring Christmas cheer to the family room at right. The table is set with 19th-century tea-leaf china.*

Made with real fleece, pull-
toy sheep like the circa 1880
German piece above were
often displayed in crèches
or under Christmas trees.
This sheep is fitted with a
bellows; when a string is
pulled, the toy sounds
a little bleat.

Holiday trimmings throughout the rest of the house are kept simple to harmonize with the understated furnishings. In the living room, for instance, the wing chair, camelback sofa, and early-18th-century Windsor chair are complemented by a few wreaths hung in the windows and by evergreen garlands on the sills. The mantelpiece is the setting for a flock of antique toy sheep, some of which were once used in elaborate Nativity scenes.

In this room, a small feather tree decorated with antique German glass ornaments stands in for a live evergreen. Still very popular, feather trees were introduced to America by German immigrants. The first artificial Christmas trees, they were traditionally made from dyed goose or

*Continued*

*A toy collection, including a flock of antique sheep on the mantel, becomes part of the Christmas decorations in the living room at left.*

*English and Irish samplers from the early 19th century, above, make an interesting backdrop for an old feather tree; the 19th-century molded and blown-glass ornaments are from Germany.*

*Among the antique toys and folk-art pieces that the homeowners have been collecting for over twenty years are the sheep and horse set out on the 18th-century maple chest of drawers above. A bow lends seasonal color to the mid-19th-century oil painting.*

turkey feathers wired to wooden dowels and were modeled after the sparse German *tannenbaum*, or silver fir. Feather trees had become common in America by the late 1800s, when a public outcry arose over the excessive cutting of evergreens that occurred at Christmas time.

Traditional decorations can also be found in the master bedroom, where the pencil-post bed is decked with greenery and bright country textiles. While the Double Irish Chain quilt that hangs behind the bed is an antique, the quilts on the bed are contemporary pieces made by a relative. Because one of the homeowners is a teacher, the appliquéd Schoolhouse quilt has particular meaning for the family. During the holidays,

*Continued*

*Garlands and a wreath form a festive "canopy" for the pencil-post tester bed at right.*

Visitors staying in the
smokehouse-turned-guest-
cottage at right awake to a
breakfast served on fine
English china. A tabletop
tree and toys nestled in
greenery bring seasonal
spirit to the room.

*An antique worksled leans against the fieldstone guest cottage above. The bell in the cupola was rescued from an old schoolhouse.*

a favorite "portrait" of a cow is accented with a simple red and green bow.

The homeowners turned the old fieldstone smokehouse (above and preceding overleaf) into a bed-and-breakfast cottage soon after purchasing the farm, and enjoy taking the time to decorate it for guests each year. Here, a tabletop tree is set on an old quilt top and trimmed with popcorn garlands and miniature lights. Along the windowsill above the bed, greens form the backdrop for favorite pieces, including a small barn and rocking horse, a papier-mâché rabbit candy container, a large pull-toy horse, and a stuffed bear from England. Simple evergreen wreaths are placed on the exterior of the guest cottage, as well as on the doors of the barn.

*The barn opposite is original to the 1844 farmstead. Completely renovated, it is now used by the homeowners for storing the antiques that they sell in a nearby shop.*

# AN OUTDOOR WREATH

**A.** The ends of two pieces of florist's wire are twisted together to make a secure loop for hanging the wreath.

Trimming a wreath is a satisfying way to herald the holidays, and it can also be surprisingly easy. To make the striking wreath opposite, designed for outdoor use, you start with a ready-made evergreen wreath. After a decorative French horn is wired on, the wreath is embellished with a loose bow looped from upholstery cording, gold-painted leaves and pinecones, and an assortment of fresh berries, greens, apples, and miniature pineapples (all of which will last for several weeks in a cold climate). To judge the balance and design, hang the wreath up after you have attached the horn; you can adjust the trimmings, which are wired to florist's picks, and vary the number you use as you like. The materials are available at florists and at Christmas shops.

## MATERIALS AND EQUIPMENT

· Ready-made fresh evergreen wreath ·
(wreath shown is about 2 feet in diameter)
· Sprigs of holly, seasonal greens, and berries · Magnolia leaves ·
· Pinecones · Miniature pineapples · Green apples ·
· Decorative French horn ·
· Upholstery cording, 4 yards each in red and gold ·
· Gold spray paint · Wooden florist's picks, 6 inches long ·
· Florist's wire · Small pruning shears ·
· Wire cutters · Scissors ·

◆

**B.** Individual trimmings are wired onto florist's picks so that they can be easily arranged on the wreath.

## DIRECTIONS

**1.** To form a loop for hanging, use the wire cutters to cut two pieces of the florist's wire, each about 18 inches long. Holding the pieces together, shape them into a large "U" and pass it from front to back through the wreath. Twist the pieces together, tightening the wire against the greens, then twist the ends to make a loop (Illustration A).

**2.** Using the pruning shears, trim the sprigs and leaves as necessary. Wire a florist's pick (which comes with wire attached) to the stem or base of each sprig and pinecone, twisting the pick to secure (Illustration B).

**3.** Spray-paint the magnolia leaves and pinecones gold.

**4.** Place the French horn on the wreath, securing it in several places with florist's wire. Hang the wreath by the wire loop.

**5.** Hold the two pieces of cording together, knot them at each end, and tie them into a loose bow. Wire the bow to a florist's pick and poke it into the wreath near the top.

**6.** Arrange the holly, seasonal greens, and berries around the wreath, inserting the picks securely, then add the magnolia leaves and pinecones.

**7.** Push each apple and pineapple onto the blunt end of a florist's pick. Place the pineapples on the wreath and secure with florist's wire. Place the apples on the wreath (Illustration C).

**C.** Secured to florist's picks, the fruits are added after the leaves, greens, and berries have been attached.

# AN INDOOR WREATH

Old-fashioned ornaments recall the spirit of Christmas Past on this pretty wreath. The Victorian paper cutouts are combined here with "tussie-mussies," or small nosegays, which are easy to make from doilies and miniature Christmas balls. To judge the balance and design, hang the wreath up before you add the trimmings; you can adjust the decorations and vary the number you use as you like. The materials are available at florists, novelty stores, and Christmas shops.

**A.** After the ribbon is wrapped around the wreath, the ends are overlapped and pinned at the top to secure them.

## MATERIALS AND EQUIPMENT

· Ready-made fresh evergreen wreath ·
(wreath shown is about 2 feet in diameter)
· About 6 yards wire-edged ribbon, 2 inches wide ·
· Paper ornaments · Miniature glass Christmas balls on wires ·
· Circular paper doilies, 6 inches in diameter ·
· Wooden florist's picks, 6 inches long · Florist's wire ·
· Dressmaker's pins · Pushpins · Wire cutters ·
· Scissors ·

◆

## DIRECTIONS

1. To form a loop for hanging, use the wire cutters to cut two pieces of the florist's wire, each about 18 inches long. Holding the pieces together, shape them into a large "U" and pass it from front to back through the wreath. Twist the pieces together, tightening the wire against the greens, then twist the ends to make a loop.

2. Wrap the ribbon around the wreath clockwise, beginning at the top front of the wreath and leaving a 2-inch tail; trim so there is a 1-inch overlap on the back. Secure the ends with one or two dressmaker's pins (Illustration A). Hang the wreath by the wire loop.

3. Make about a dozen tussie-mussies. For each, hold four Christmas balls together and insert their wires through the center of a doily; pinch the doily and twist it to gather it around the balls. Using the wire cutters, trim the wires 2 inches below the doily (Illustration B). Wire a florist's pick (which comes with wire attached) to the bottom of each tussie-mussie, twisting the pick to secure.

4. Cut a 1-yard length of ribbon; pull it through the center of the wreath at the top and align the ends to make a loop. Using a pushpin, temporarily pin the ends out of the way above the wreath. Make a generous bow from lengths of the remaining ribbon, using florist's wire or dressmaker's pins to secure the loops and soft center puff.

5. Arrange the tussie-mussies on the wreath, inserting the florist's picks to secure. Add the ornaments, tucking some into the greenery.

6. Hold the bow over the ribbon hanging loop to see where it looks best. Reposition the pushpin to secure the hanging loop at this point, then cut any excess ribbon above the pushpin. Place the bow over the pushpin and secure with a dressmaker's pin (Illustration C).

**B.** The tussie-mussies are made from glass balls and paper doilies, then wired onto florist's picks for easy arranging.

**C.** The wreath is hung by a sturdy wire loop camouflaged by ribbon; a decorative bow is added last.

# Holiday Elegance

The sunny garden room at right, overlooking a sweeping valley, is decorated with an abundance of natural greenery. "Each year we add more and more," says a family member, who gathered the pine boughs from the property.

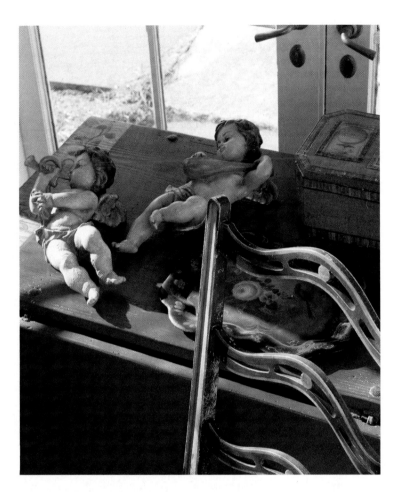

Every year, this hillside home in the Berkshire Mountains of Massachusetts becomes the setting for a joyous country Christmas with decorations that are simple yet elegant.

In one of two sunny garden rooms, for example, the French doors are effectively crowned with swags of laurel, hemlock, and spruce, and are trimmed with lush pinecone-studded evergreen wreaths. The focal point of the decorations, however, is the dramatic tree, often as tall as fourteen feet, placed in the curve of the elegant living room staircase (overleaf), where it rises all the way to the second floor landing. The majestic tree is decorated generously, and all sorts of ornaments, from glass balls to a multitude of hearts—crafted in glass, wood, metal, and paper—find a place on the branches. "We

*Continued*

*Collected on the homeowners'*
*travels, the* putti *above,*
*set on an 18th-century*
*Swedish table in the garden*
*room, are contemporary*
*Italian reproductions*
*made of polychrome wood.*
*Such celestial figures were*
*common in Renaissance*
*art, and often appeared*
*in European Nativity*
*scenes in the 1700s.*

Made of wood and decorated
with metallic paints, the
small winged cherub face
above — a copy of an 18th-
century Spanish piece —
is from Barcelona.

*Garlands draped along
the curving banister
frame the fourteen-foot
tree in the living
room at left.*

*On the living room table at right, a poinsettia in full blossom calls attention to a collection of silver, porcelain, and cloisonné boxes. Nearby, a papier-mâché reindeer peeks from behind a comfortable armchair.*

have been collecting ornaments for more than forty years and buy them everywhere, looking for all periods and types," say the homeowners. "Friends also give them to us each year."

Found throughout the living room are surprising, original seasonal touches. A pressed-glass compote filled with small red glass balls that resemble bunches of grapes, for example, makes an unusual and striking accessory on an antique candlestand, while papier-mâché angels take flight from pine roping atop a gilded 19th-century mirror. A large poinsettia and whimsical papier-mâché reindeer dressed with a red bow decorate a cozy conversation area near the fireplace, and a painted tea table showcases a collection of bottle brush trees and members of the owners' many Christmas "orchestras"—frosted-glass angels made in Europe.

*A turn-of-the-century painted leather screen from Italy forms the backdrop for the Christmas*

*vignette above. The imaginative grouping includes brass candlesticks, bottle brush trees,*

*and frosted-glass angels playing musical instruments.*

# ROMANTIC GIFT WRAPS

Everyone appreciates a surprise at Christmas, and special gift wraps add to the pleasure. The well-dressed packages here and on the following pages will give you some imaginative ideas for wrappings that will be as memorable as your gifts.

The packages at right convey a romantic, old-fashioned feeling. Papers, fabrics, ribbons, and trims for wrapping presents like these can come from many different sources, such as art supply, decorating, and fabric shops. For a particularly rich look, try overwrapping gifts with two layers of paper or fabric. A sheet of lacy rice paper or a piece of sheer organdy or tulle is effective over dark-toned metallic paper. Or, use a narrow wallpaper border as an elegant trim on contrasting, solid-color paper.

Devoting some thought to the gift-recipient's hobbies and interests will help you make creative use of your supplies. A bouquet of dried roses, for instance, is the perfect trim for a flower-lover's present. An artist or craftsperson might appreciate a package done up in handmade marbleized paper, while wallpaper makes an appropriate wrap for a gift to someone who is redecorating.

The dressed-up packages at right are almost too pretty to open. On some, the tops and bottoms are wrapped separately so that the decorated boxes can be reused.

# CASUAL
# GIFT WRAPS

The casual gift wrappings at left, most of which are created from paper and other supplies that might be found around the house, make great family projects. Ordinary craft and construction papers, for example, are easily transformed into Christmas wrappings with sponge printing. Simply cut clean, dry sponges into various shapes with sharp scissors, or use a firm apple or pear sliced in half. Daub the sponge or fruit in acrylic paint and print.

Large envelopes can be dressed up with stickers and ribbons, and paper bags make convenient wrappings for cookies and other Christmas baked goods. Use rubber stamps to decorate the bags with repeat patterns. Or, cut the tops of the bags into scalloped borders and embellish them with paper-punch designs. You can then make a row of paper-punch holes or small slits and weave ribbon, raffia, or yarn through the openings.

Some wraps might also be part of the gift. Linen towels secured with ribbon, for example, make lively—and useful—packages. And for a small gift, a handmade fabric bag with a drawstring tie is a good alternative to a box; the bag can then be filled with potpourri and reused by the recipient as a sachet.

The fabric scraps, paper bags, envelopes, and other household items at left are trimmed with decorative stickers and ribbons to create innovative Christmas wrappings.

# A Christmas Showcase

This brick and fieldstone Pennsylvania farmhouse, built in two parts during the 18th century, is a showcase for the present owners' antiques and Christmas decorations. Because one family member's birthday falls in December, the holidays have become a dual celebration that continues to grow in scope.

The owners search for new Christmas decorating ideas throughout the year and begin to ready the house for the yuletide season just after Thanksgiving. Several trees are set up, and the entire house is filled with Santas and

*The family that live in the historic Pennsylvania house at left are descendants of the original Quaker owners. The brick portion was built in 1705 and the field-stone addition dates from 1783.*

bearded gnomes known as Belsnickels (an extensive collection of Christmas figures, both old and new, numbers over three hundred). "Friends started giving me Santas and ornaments for my birthday," explains one homeowner, "and it all just evolved from there."

Santas, however, are only the beginning; the family also decorate with imaginative arrangements of antiques, grouping sleds and baby carriages under the various trees and placing toys and folk-art pieces on mantels and windowsills. Food also plays a role: pretzels, dried fruits, and

*Continued*

*Dominated by the original walk-in fireplace, the family room at right is particularly inviting at holiday time. Bottle brush trees from the 1920s and vintage Santas adorn the mantel.*

homemade cookies are fashioned into ornaments and garlands.

As a result, each room has its own warm character. Located in the late-18th-century stone section of the house, the family room (preceding overleaf) is decorated informally to enhance its cozy atmosphere. Here, the tree is trimmed especially to appeal to children. This entails using a variety of homemade edible ornaments—strings of dark and golden raisins, gin-gerbread cookies, sand tarts, popcorn garlands, and pretzel rings. While beeswax candles are fastened to the branches, the tapers are not actually lit; instead, the homeowners use tiny white lights to simulate the glow of candlelight.

The tree in the dining room at right is decorated more formally, and with a Victorian flair. Trimming a tree with flags was particularly popular in the late 19th century, and the tradition is recalled here with American flags found in a

*Continued*

*Dried flowers, including cockscomb and Queen Anne's lace, as well as flags (probably made in the 1940s)
and candles, decorate the distinctive dining room tree above and at right. The doll carriage and
"belly" sled underneath date from the 1860s.*

First used around 1878, counterweight candleholders, or candle bobs, like the 1890s examples above, were designed to hang on tree branches. The bodies of the angel and Santa are weighted to keep the candles upright.

A kissing ball—a popular Christmas decoration in Victorian times—hangs from the chandelier in the breakfast room at right. Homemade from dried mistletoe, evergreens, and flowers, it is saved and used year after year.

summer house many years ago. The homeowners have also added flowers picked from their own garden earlier in the year and then dried: fuzzy cockscomb, yellow yarrow, delicate clusters of Queen Anne's lace, starflowers, lavender, roses, and salvia. The other ornaments include dried pomegranates strung on red cord, tin icicles, and candle bobs.

The breakfast room at left is part of a wing added to the house in 1970. This informal dining area is appropriately decorated with Christmas edibles. Gingerbread men are lined up along a swing-up bar grate, which is also trimmed with a chain of dried apple slices set off by greenery. In a window, more apple slices are gathered with twine into miniature wreaths, while little bundles of two or three cinnamon sticks are tied up with red yarn. The chain is made from apples and filberts strung on a wire and finished off with a pretty plaid bow. *Continued*

*Set atop a 19th-century blanket chest, the breakfast room tree above features ornaments relating to the goat, the family "mascot." The ceramic Santa Claus mugs displayed beneath the tree date from the 1930s.*

Also in the breakfast room is the "goat tree." Because one of the owners grew up on a horse farm where goats were kept to calm the skittish thoroughbreds, the goat has been adopted as a whimsical family mascot. Each year, a small tabletop tree is decorated with 19th-century tin, wooden, and ceramic toy goats from their collection, and with related items such as bundles of hay bound with string and little fences homemade from matchsticks. The tiny wreath atop the tree even features a small, wooden goat's head inside it.

Christmas spirit is also extended to the bedrooms. In the guest room above and at right, a group of wooden Santa figures find a place on the mantelpiece, while a 19th-century rocking horse and a contemporary carved Santa stand by the hearth. Hanging from the feather tree in the window are wooden Noah's ark animals. And on the Victorian dressing table, the homeowners have set up a festive holiday "tea party," complete with miniature furniture, stuffed bears, a doll's tea set—and even a tiny feather tree centerpiece.

*Stockings made from old quilt fragments are hung by the chimney with care in the guest room above.*
*The warm country feeling in the room is enhanced by the collection of well-loved antique toys at right,*
*including a Victorian-era stuffed bear and 1920s pull-toy dog.*

The egg-shaped Santa above, known as a roly-poly, was made as a toy; when it is tipped over, it pops right back up. The piece was produced around 1910 by the Schoenhut toy factory of Philadelphia, which manufactured many different roly-poly Santas.

# SPICY FRUIT POMANDERS

Originally small filigree balls of gold, silver, or ivory filled with fragrant spices and an ambergris fixative, pomanders (from the French *pomme d'ambre,* or apple of ambergris) were used as early as the Middle Ages, when they were worn to ward off unpleasant odors. Today's version of the pomander is made by studding a piece of fruit with cloves and curing it in a mixture of ground spices with orrisroot as a fixative.

Pomanders are lovely holiday gifts.

Not only do they make fragrant decorations that can be hung from ribbons or arranged in bowls, but when placed in closets, they help keep woolens moth-free.

A pomander's scent usually lasts for several years, but can be refreshed by dipping the pomander in warm water, then rolling it in fresh spices to which a drop or two of cinnamon or clove oil has been added. Leave the pomander in the mixture for a few days, then use as before.

## MATERIALS AND EQUIPMENT

· 6 to 8 assorted firm, thin-skinned apples, oranges, lemons, and limes ·

· ½ pound whole, large-headed cloves with strong scent ·

· ¼ cup ground cinnamon · ¼ cup ground cloves ·

· 2 tablespoons ground nutmeg ·

· 2 tablespoons ground allspice · ¼ cup powdered orrisroot ·

· Nut pick or slender knitting needle for piercing fruit (optional) ·

· Ribbon (optional) · Small paintbrush ·

◆

## ASSEMBLY

**1.** Hold a piece of the fruit firmly, without squeezing. Insert the cloves at ⅛- to ¼-inch intervals in rows (or at random) over the surface; the fruit will shrink as it dries, closing up the spaces. (If you have difficulty inserting the cloves, you can pierce the fruit first with the point of a nut pick or knitting needle, but take care to keep the holes small or the cloves will fall out when the fruit dries.) If you intend to hang your pomanders from ribbons, you can leave a 1-inch "path" around the fruit to provide a channel to keep the ribbon in place.

**2.** Blend the spices and orrisroot in a small bowl. One at a time, roll each piece of fruit in the mixture, coating it generously to keep air out. (Any pomander you start should be completed to this point within twenty-four hours to eliminate the possibility of mold forming.)

**3.** Place the spice-coated fruit in a large bowl, cover with the spice mixture, and set in a warm, dry place to dry. Turn the fruit daily, making sure the spices are evenly distributed. Drying can take from two weeks to a month, depending on the size of the fruit. The pomanders will be hard when they are completely dry.

**4.** Remove the pomanders from the spice mixture and dust off the excess with the brush. Tie with ribbon, if desired.

# Christmas
# Past

The owners of this late-19th-century house believe in preserving the past. Abandoning city life in the 1970s, they purchased a neglected farmstead at auction and renovated and enlarged the old house themselves. Their appreciation of history extends not only to the carefully chosen furnishings that now fill the house, but also to their Christmas decorations, which include toys, feather trees, and a collection of antique ornaments.

To show off their favorite ornaments—kugels, wax angels, printed paper "scraps," and chains

*Continued*

*Crafted by a family member, the feather tree above is designed with branches on only two sides so that it can be easily placed against a window or wall. The brass wreath is made from animal, tree, sleigh, and angel shapes cast from old candy molds.*

*On the family room mantelpiece at left, Santas handcrafted by a friend appear to tend German toy sheep. The vine wreaths are homemade.*

of colorful glass beads made in 19th-century Germany and Czechoslovakia—the homeowners specifically choose a balsam tree for its short needles and long, well-spaced branches. "We used to cut down our own tree every year and always looked for one with an old bird's nest in it," recalls one family member. "Now we buy a tree and put a nest in it ourselves."

Favoring natural materials and fresh greenery, the family also craft many of their decorations, which include grapevine wreaths for the family room (preceding overleaf). These might be trimmed with antique toys, spun-cotton fruits, pinecones, and fresh cedar sprigs. Hand-made as well are a number of feather trees, crafted from dyed goose feathers and displayed throughout the house. Such holiday finery may even be found in the sewing room, where an antique feather tree twinkles with bead chains; gathered like presents around its base are a roly-poly Santa, antique dolls, and one of the many miniature sewing machines in the homeowners' collection.

Cooking is also an important part of the family's holiday celebration, and many of their kitchen collectibles, including vintage cookie cutters, are pressed into service for Christmas baking. In the cozy kitchen are simple decorations such

*Continued*

*During the 19th and early 20th centuries, many pincushions were designed to be ornamental and were often given as gifts. Cushions like the beaded velvet piece, top, which may have been made by American Indians for trade in the early 1900s, and the Victorian-era boot, bottom, are now popular collectibles.*

*In addition to sewing machines, lace—stored on old bobbins in the sewing room opposite—and pincushions, including the beaded pieces from the 1890s on the windowsill above, are collected by the homeowners. The framed work is a German house blessing spelled out in pins.*

*Fresh greenery, rolling pins and cutting boards, and a pinecone wreath studded with spun-cotton fruits make a charming Christmas still life in a corner of the kitchen.*

as greenery and pinecone wreaths; here, evergreen sprays sprout from an old chicken scale and a few bright red apples nest in a bed of pine. Like the trimmings in the rest of the house, these seasonal touches have an informal, comfortable character. "We don't consciously follow any one holiday decorating scheme," say the owners. "We've always collected old things and just enjoy using what we have."

*Shiny apples and a few sprigs of pine bring yuletide cheer to this country kitchen; vintage utensils still come in handy for holiday baking.*

# ELEGANT TRUFFLES

Truffles are not hard to make, but the chocolate can get soft and sticky when you are working with it, so be sure that your kitchen is not excessively hot—and work quickly. The finished truffles should be stored in the refrigerator, between layers of wax paper in an airtight container. If you cover the container with plastic wrap and then with foil, the sweets will keep for up to two weeks in the refrigerator or two months in the freezer. To defrost, thaw overnight in the refrigerator.

## BASIC CHOCOLATE TRUFFLES

½ cup heavy cream
¼ cup unsalted butter
Pinch salt
8 ounces semisweet or bittersweet
   chocolate, in pieces
1 teaspoon vanilla extract

2 tablespoons unsweetened
   cocoa powder
2 tablespoons confectioners'
   sugar, plus additional
   for coating

1. In small saucepan, warm cream, butter, and salt over low heat just until butter is melted.

2. Stir in chocolate. Reduce heat to very low and cook, stirring, until chocolate is melted and smooth. Remove from heat and stir in vanilla. Pour mixture into medium bowl, cover with plastic wrap, and refrigerate until firm, about 3 hours.

3. Shape and coat truffles: In small bowl, mix together cocoa and 2 tablespoons of the confectioners' sugar. Place bowl of chocolate in larger bowl of ice and water to keep mixture firm. Using melon baller or 2 teaspoons, dipped in confectioners' sugar, scoop some chilled chocolate into small ball. Roll ball in cocoa-sugar mixture. (You can also sprinkle your fingers and palms with confectioners' sugar and shape mixture by hand, but work quickly to keep chocolate from melting.)

4. After coating each truffle, place in small fluted paper candy cup and keep refrigerated. Let truffles stand at room temperature for 10 to 15 minutes before serving; do not let them remain at room temperature for very long or they will become too soft.　　　　　Makes 4 dozen

**Flavor variations:** You can alter the basic truffle recipe above by adding flavorings such as these:

◆ Rum Raisin: Into the melted chocolate, stir ¼ cup chopped golden raisins that have been soaked for 30 minutes in ¼ cup warmed dark rum and then drained. You can also stir in the rum if you like.
◆ Coffee Kahlua: Stir ¼ cup Kahlua and 1 tablespoon instant espresso powder into the cream and melted butter before adding the chocolate.
◆ Orange: Stir 1 tablespoon grated orange zest and ½ teaspoon orange extract into the melted chocolate.

**Coating variations:** In addition to flavoring the truffles, try rolling them in any of the following: toasted flaked coconut; chopped almonds or pistachios; plain granulated sugar, or ¾ cup granulated sugar tossed with 2 teaspoons grated orange zest that has been patted dry.

*Few toys found under the tree on Christmas morning make a child happier than a train set. The tin locomotive above was produced by the Günthermann Company of Nuremberg, Germany, in the early 1900s.*

# A Victorian Celebration

The spirit of a Victorian Christmas pervades this Philadelphia house designed in the Queen Anne style. Built in the 1890s, the stately residence was renovated and decorated to period by its current owners, who stripped down the woodwork and carefully chose the Victorian wallpapers, fixtures, and furniture. "When it came time to celebrate our first Christmas in the house, it was only natural to decorate for the holiday in Victorian style as well," they explain.

The focus of the family's Christmas decor is a balsam fir, which they place in the entrance hall so that it can be seen from all the first-floor rooms. The fragrant tree is trimmed with a mix of ornaments, including family heirlooms, as well as period reproductions and homemade pieces; in Victorian fashion, the tree is set on a table.

Other traditional Victorian Christmas decorations—kissing balls and a winter tree—are found in the living room. Kissing balls, also

*Continued*

*The stained-glass window above, original to the 1890s house, forms a colorful backdrop for an arrangement of toys: a 1940s train set, a tin fire engine, and a 19th-century cast-iron dog.*

*Many decorations in this Victorian house are sentimental favorites. The village nestled beneath the tree opposite was made by one of the homeowners when he was a child, while the tinfoil star at the top of the tree is a memento from the couple's first Christmas together.*

known as kissing boughs or bunches, were usually made by wrapping wooden hoops with mistletoe, holly, or other greens (this family make theirs from boxwood), and sometimes adding ribbons and paper rosettes. According to English custom, the balls were hung, perhaps over a doorway or loveseat, as an invitation to kiss.

The winter tree, above, recalls the Victorian tradition of preserving a Christmas tree from

*Continued*

*Painted white, the elegant "winter tree" above, made from a tree top, is decorated with homemade clay ornaments that were shaped with cookie cutters.*

*Festoons of boxwood follow the soft draping of the curtains in the living room at left. Dried statice and heather adorn a small tabletop tree.*

*The dried and bleached ferns above have the fragile appearance of snowflakes. Pinecones, porcelain dolls, and a candle complete the imaginative vignette.*

year to year. After the holiday celebrations were over, it was the practice of some people—particularly German settlers in Pennsylvania—to strip the tree of its needles and store the skeleton; the following Christmas, the boughs would be wrapped in cotton batting to simulate snow and the tree redecorated. By the early 1900s, when the natural supply of evergreens was dwindling, it was not unusual for barren trees to be cut down, brought inside, and decorated with batting in the same manner. In lieu of cotton batting, the winter tree made by this family was simply sprayed with white paint. The same frosty look characterizes the dried and bleached ferns that decorate the windowsill above. A larger windowsill display appears in the bedroom at right. Here, a collection of dolls belonging to one of the homeowners, including many favorites that have been passed down through generations, is grouped with poinsettias and greens.

*A kissing ball, evergreen boughs, and red and white poinsettias bring a festive look to the Victorian-style bedroom at right.*

# MAKING CORNUCOPIAS

F illed with popcorn, candy, fruit, or nuts, paper cornucopias like those above once found a popular place on the Christmas tree. Directions for making these small containers appeared in late-19th-century ladies' magazines. At that time, candy and "sweetmeats" played an important holiday role; these inexpensive gifts were eagerly awaited by children, who were seldom given the opportunity to feast on such treats during the rest of the year.

Cornucopias still make festive ornaments and are easy to craft. You will need lightweight cardboard for a pattern, decorative papers (wrapping paper is fine), trims (try stickers, braid, sequins, and fancy ribbons), craft glue, spray adhesive, a drafting compass, and scissors.

Begin by using the compass to draft a quarter-circle pattern onto lightweight cardboard (the cornucopias shown here have a radius of 4, 5, or 6 inches). On one straight edge of the pattern add a ¼-inch-wide overlap allowance, then taper the allowance at the point; cut the pattern out.

For each cornucopia, trace the pattern onto a piece of decorative paper and cut to make the outside piece; then reverse the pattern and repeat to make a lining. On the wrong sides, spray the paper pieces with adhesive and stick them together. Apply the craft glue to the allowance on the outside paper, then roll the paper into a cone. Trim as desired. Glue a piece of ribbon to the inside rim for a handle and cover the ends with a band of trim.

# Holiday Artistry

*Simple garlands, handmade Santas, and a collection of feather trees decorate the family room, right. A twig fence surrounds the group of trees on the chest. Such fences were popular under-the-tree decorations beginning in the late 1800s and usually enclosed a village, Nativity, or farm scene.*

The owners of this 1860s Wisconsin farmhouse blend the furnishings and Christmas collectibles they have acquired over time with newly crafted ornaments for an original holiday decor. One of the homeowners is an artist and dollmaker who spends several months each year preparing for a local Christmas crafts fair; her own Santas and folk figures, as well as other pieces made by friends, have particular personal meaning.

Rather than concentrating their efforts in any one room, the family enjoy decorating the entire house, favoring vignettes of antique toys or single folk-art pieces trimmed with a bit of greenery. The simplicity of the decorations—a garland strung over a window or from a beam—is especially well suited to the homey look of the old house, and the arrangements can be easily changed according to the family's whims.

*Continued*

*An angel doll, above, crafted by one of the homeowners, sits comfortably inside a distinctive wreath made of cedar, pinecones, cinnamon sticks, and berries. Completing this family room scene are a selection of pieces collected over the years: a vintage pencil box, a tin car from the 1920s, and a mechanical bank.*

*Decorated with winter scenes, tins once used to package cookies, candies, and other Christmas treats make cheerful decorations long after their edible contents have disappeared. The square box, top, is an English biscuit tin; the round tin, bottom, made in America around the 1950s, held fruitcake.*

The antique furnishings, gathered over the years from local shops or discovered at flea markets, also become a natural part of the Christmas decorating scheme. In the family room, for example, an old log sled and a newspaper delivery wagon serve as the settings for homemade holiday treats and a tea party for two handcrafted bears.

Most arrangements incorporate feather trees from the family's extensive collection, which includes antiques and reproductions in many sizes. They appear throughout the house, atop tables and chests or clustered on windowsills.

Some of the feather trees are trimmed with simple red berry ornaments—a berry or candleholder at the tip of each branch was the German custom—while others are left plain. The largest of the feather trees displayed in the family room is decorated with cherry-shaped candies strung on wires, papier-mâché stars, and anise-flavored candy rings.

Another feather tree, an antique, is set on a butcher block to provide Christmas cheer in a corner of the kitchen, opposite. Arranged as "gifts" around its base and on the floor is a prized collection of vintage food tins. A second

*Continued*

*Above, the pine refectory table in the kitchen is set with an antique tea-leaf ironstone coffeepot and the family's heirloom Christmas china—a red-and-green floral pattern by Johnson Brothers, an English porcelain firm.*

*A turn-of-the-century addition to the 1860s house, the kitchen is decorated for the yuletide season. Opposite, an antique feather tree strung with garlands of tiny stars sits atop a butcherblock surrounded by a collection of vintage food tins.*

*Many childhood treasures*
*have been used to decorate*
*the upstairs hallway at right*
*for the holidays. Among the*
*children's books displayed*
*on the log beam is one*
*about Saint Nicholas.*

grouping of tins set out on a dry sink is trimmed with evergreen sprigs, candy canes, and pinecones. Above the sink hang a trio of tiny straw wreaths dressed up for Christmas.

Even out-of-the-way spaces like the upstairs hallway above get special attention. Here, looking as though it would be the perfect spot for a child to await Santa's arrival, a small rocking bed, covered with a feather ticking and a Log Cabin quilt, is tucked into the corner. A pine garland hangs from the beam above the bed, as do handmade stockings sewn from a crazy patchwork of velvet and antique lace remnants. A collection of toys, including dolls and trains, as well as children's books, is lined up along the top of the beam, and an old chalkboard mounted on the wall proclaims the family's good wishes for the holiday season.

# CREATIVE IDEAS FOR
# THE CHRISTMAS SEASON

◆ If you are an overnight guest, tuck small thank-you gifts into cupboards, nooks, and crannies; your hosts will enjoy finding them and will recall your stay with pleasure.

◆ Reword a holiday poem or carol to be read aloud; try "The Twelve Days of Christmas" set in the present.

◆ Use plain paper tablecloths for a children's party. Place crayons at each setting and let the small folk draw and sign holiday pictures.

◆ Stage a winter barbecue and have a snowman-building contest while the food is cooking.

◆ Hold a family-history party. Ask relatives to bring old photo albums to a holiday gathering and enjoy sharing times gone by.

◆ Make a scrapbook guest register. Keep Christmas stickers, trims, ribbons, doilies, and glue handy and ask each visitor to decorate a page.

◆ Ask guests to sign 6-inch lengths of grosgrain ribbon with a glitter pen, then glue the pieces into a memory chain for your tree.

◆ Trim a pretty green houseplant to use as a tabletop tree. Decorate it with small red bows and tiny white lights; wrap the pot in gift paper.

◆ Bring a Christmas "picnic" to an elderly or housebound neighbor.

◆ Make paper-doll-style garlands to trim shelves, a mantel, or an archway; depict family members or choose seasonal images.

◆ When wrapping gifts, include a "clue" to encourage recipients to try to guess the contents.

◆ Attach a small ornament to the package wrapping; it will bring back memories each time the recipient hangs it on the tree.

◆ Use images cut from old Christmas cards to make gift tags that can be hung on the tree once the packages are opened.

◆ Trim an outdoor tree or wreath with food for the birds; be prepared to replenish it often!

◆ Don't forget the four-footed family members. Wrap a wreath with ribbon and tuck in dog biscuits; trim another with catnip mice and jingle-bell toys to put your felines in the holiday spirit.

# A Collector's Christmas

N ew and vintage folk art—cleverly arranged by an enthusiastic collector—distinguishes the Christmas decor in this Pennsylvania home. Built in the mid-18th century, the historic structure has housed a saddlery, a tavern, and several general stores over the years. Part of the building is still used as a country store by the present owners; instead of seed and overalls, however, the shopkeepers now purvey folk art pieces, as well as antique and reproduction country furnishings.

The living quarters of the building have been carefully renovated to provide an appropriate backdrop for the family's antiques and collections. Christmas decorating starts the day after Thanksgiving in the keeping room, a combination kitchen and family room (left and overleaf) that the homeowners created by removing a partition. "Since we've been here ten years, I pretty much know the areas I want to decorate," says one family member, "but I like to change the materials and look each year." Because it is a large space, a number of small groupings are planned throughout the room; many include contemporary folk-art decorations from the owners' store.

The setup shown here features Santa figures parading across the kitchen island (cotton batting provides a snowy ground beneath them).

*Continued*

*Fragrant and pretty, fresh greens—including fir, juniper, holly, and delicate sprigs of cedar—are tucked here and there in the keeping room, left.*

The ceiling-high tree in the keeping room is decorated with contemporary folk-art ornaments; whimsical trinkets also find a place on the boughs. Branches of pine and red-berried holly are arranged on tables and windowsills. Dried pomegranates nest in greenery atop the window sashes.

The mantelpiece across the room has become a Christmas homestead, complete with an antique miniature log cabin, farm animals, and a tiny woodpile. The homeowners also take advantage of the space offered by the deep-set windows in the room, varying the arrangements on each sill. On one, a few pieces of redware crockery are joined by some berry-sprigged branches to make a casual but striking still life, while on the other, handcrafted Santas and an assortment of farm animal figures appear to have gathered for their own celebration.

The focal point of the room, however, is the nearly ten-foot-tall tree. The ornaments, which are all contemporary pieces, are a colorful mix of traditional glass balls, Santas, and gingerbread men, as well as miniature baskets, tin quilt motifs, cardboard folk-art figures, and even a scherenschnitt Noah's ark; a smiling rag-doll angel is placed at the top. To emphasize the country look of the tree even more, the base has been turned into a whimsical farmyard scene where toy sheep, pigs, and a cow graze together on a bed of hay.  *Continued*

*The collection of contemporary handcrafted Santas above includes a tall, brown-suited figure made from clay and a stuffed-cotton piece emerging from a wooden "brick" chimney. The small cedar tree is decked with lamb's-wool sheep, clay stars and hearts, tin stars, and white tallow berries.*

*The cheerful red-and-green color scheme of the guest room at right provides the perfect backdrop for Christmas decorations. The country wreath is made from rose hips.*

*A small Fraser fir suits the cozy bedroom above. The figure of the little girl is a reproduction of a dummy board.*

In contrast to the first-floor keeping room, the upstairs bedrooms are decorated very simply. In a guest room (preceding overleaf), a red-and-white quilt is brought out each year to provide Christmas color. Princess pine roping entwined with popcorn frames the peg rack and door, and sugar-cookie men hang from the garland.

In another bedroom, above and opposite, the setting features a small fir tree trimmed with red ribbon bows, dried apple slices, cinnamon hearts, rose hips, and shortbread cookies. Lace collars and sprigs of holly tucked into the three-tiered wall basket over the bed add an especially festive note.

*Tucking a few evergreen boughs and some branches of holly around a collection of bandboxes was all it took to create the striking Christmas vignette atop the wardrobe opposite. An antique tin monkey jumping jack hangs from the latch. The Noah's ark is a contemporary work.*

# Regional Holiday Style

## *celebrating Christmas around the country*

Tis chapter presents four houses located in four different parts of the country. In decorating these homes, the owners have recalled the rich histories of their regions with indigenous furnishings, folk art, and textiles, both old and new.

At holiday time, many of the trimmings are chosen with particular respect for the location and style of the house. Angel and star ornaments inspired by the images in German frakturs, for example, appear on a tree in a Pennsylvania residence. Native cedar and yaupon, as well as grapevines, are gathered for the garlands and wreaths that deck a Texas farmhouse. In New Mexico, red-chili wreaths and Mexican candelabra complement the bright decor of an adobe house. And in a restored 18th-century Connecticut farmhouse, a freshly cut fir tree trimmed with hand-dipped candles is among the simple, natural decorations chosen for a New England celebration. Many of these ideas can be adapted for decorating a house in any part of the country. Moreover, they may inspire you to explore and celebrate the colorful holiday traditions of your own region.

*Clay figures and a red-chili wreath enliven a New Mexico home.*

# A Warm Connecticut Christmas

*Until the late 19th century, cookie cutters like the one above, shaped as Santa with his pack, were made from narrow strips of tin that were bent into fanciful forms and soldered to a tin backing; some five hundred different designs are known to exist.*

Each room in this 1744 Connecticut farm-house, decked out for the holidays, reflects a strong appreciation for colonial New England craftsmanship. Since restoring the house some thirty years ago, the owners have filled it with Connecticut and Massachusetts antiques that date from the late 1600s to about 1790. Many of the furnishings were made locally and represent some of the best workmanship of their time, and nearly every one has a tale of discovery associated with it.

At Christmas time, the decorations and prepa-rations also reveal a fascination with history. In each room, the flicker of candlelight contributes to the sense of time gone by. All of the candles are hand-dipped by one of the homeowners, who has taught country crafts such as can-dlemaking at the farm. "I prefer the colors I am able to achieve by dipping to those of candles that can be found in the stores," she says.

To maintain the early look of the house, the various holiday trimmings are intentionally kept simple but cheerful. "The first colonists did not decorate at Christmas," the owner explains, "but they did use a lot of color in their homes." For a homespun, natural look, fragrant garlands of pine embellished with little more than a few apples, pinecones, or dried pomegranates are favored.

All of the greens—holly, boxwood, white

*Continued*

*Tiny tree lights and hand-dipped candles create soft lighting in this farmhouse parlor at Christmas.*
*Carefully chosen antiques include the country Queen Anne desk from Connecticut, left. The fireplace lintel*
*above was carved when a prosperous farmer, Colonel Samuel Clark, owned the house.*

Simple touches of greenery add holiday spirit to the old kitchen—now used as a living room. Restored to working order by the owners, the large fireplace had been covered over with boards and bricks. The unusual 17th-century chair in the foreground, a prized piece, has an angel-and-heart design carved into its crest, and is thought to have been made as a wedding gift for its original owner, Metta Hauschildt.

pine, laurel leaves, as well as a fir tree—come from the farm. Sparkling with tiny white lights, the handsome tree is set up in the parlor and decorated with baby's-breath and achillea (some of which is dyed a rosy color), picked from the homeowners' garden, and with home-baked ginger-cookie hearts shaped with an old tin cookie cutter. "Gathering greenery and making the decorations are half the joy of Christmas," says one owner. Also welcome are decorations made by friends, such as the small ivy topiary—trained over a chicken-wire base—that are placed on the hearth in the old kitchen (preceding overleaf).

Holiday trimmings also appear in the master bedroom, where—played off against the colors of the painted woodwork and antique textiles—they create a feeling of warmth that offsets the chill New England light. Baskets of poinsettias set on a bench provide Christmas color at the foot of the bed. And on a drop-leaf table by the windows, Japanese andromeda, white pine, and black alder twigs with bright red berries make a simple but effective arrangement.

*Federal-period antiques in the master bedroom include the field bed at left and the mirror above, a Massachusetts piece distinguished by a gold frame and reverse painting on glass. The graceful Queen Anne drop-leaf table, from Connecticut, has been in the family since the 1700s.*

# HISTORY OF THE CHRISTMAS TREE

The tradition of the Christmas tree as we know it today is a relatively new one, first becoming widespread only in the 1800s. Yet it represents the influence of countless folk traditions and has roots extending to ancient times. Considered magical for their promise of life in the dead of winter, evergreens had particular significance in ancient pagan cultures, and by the Middle Ages had taken on meaning in the Christian religion. Greens were incorporated into medieval miracle plays based on Bible stories. During the Christmas season, a play honoring Adam and Eve was traditionally presented; an evergreen hung with apples, the fruit of knowledge, was the principal stage property. Villagers began imitating this "paradise" tree by decorating their own trees with apples, and the tradition continued long after the plays had disappeared.

Today's Christmas tree is probably the descendant of this paradise tree and of the German *lichtstock*—a wooden pyramid trimmed with evergreen sprigs, Nativity figures, and candles—that still appears in certain regions in Europe. At some point in time people began using the lichtstock candles on trees as well. One legend holds that Martin Luther introduced the lighted tree in the 1500s; supposedly, he was so taken

with the beauty of the night sky during a Christmas Eve walk that he brought home an evergreen for his children and decorated it with candles to simulate twinkling stars. A 19th-century painting of the scene helped to popularize the custom.

Christmas trees became increasingly common in Europe from the late 1700s onward and the tradition came to America with German settlers in the early 1800s. The tree really caught on in this country in 1850, when a newspaper illustration of Queen Victoria's lavishly ornamented tree at Windsor Castle was reprinted in America. Admirers of the royal family sought to imitate the scene in their own homes, decorating their trees with fruits, cookies, nuts, and paper flowers. It was not until the 1870s that commercially made ornaments were available in America.

**Clockwise from upper left:** a 1916 tinsel-decorated German Christmas tree; one of the earliest known depictions of an American Christmas tree, c. 1817; an English tree being topped with the Union Jack in 1876; an 1845 painting of Martin Luther and his candlelit tree; decorating the tree in the 1940s; Queen Victoria and Prince Albert display their tabletop tree at Windsor Castle in 1848; a tumbleweed tree in an Arizona schoolroom in 1907; a 1905 tree trimmed with candles and glass balls; German trees decorated with molded sugar-and-egg confections in the early 1800s.

# Pennsylvania Celebrations

When Benjamin Stauffer, a successful physician, built this distinctive red-brick house in rural Pennsylvania in 1848, he probably hoped to impress his neighbors. But while the elegant design of the front door and roof cornice gave his home the look of an imposing town house, the rooms inside, with their high ceilings, simple moldings, and painted trim, were still in keeping with the unaffected feeling of a country setting.

In restoring the house, the present owners have intentionally preserved the mix of refinement and small-town Pennsylvania charm that Dr. Stauffer built in. The couple have furnished the house with country antiques—painted cupboards, Windsor chairs, and walnut tables—

*Continued*

*Balsam garlands deck the front hall staircase above. The 1800s tall clock was made by Emanuel Meily, a Pennsylvania weaver who also excelled at cabinetmaking.*

*Garlands and a wreath decorate the Greek Revival doorway of the Pennsylvania farmhouse opposite.*

The old summer kitchen at right now serves as a casual living room. The small tree in the window is decorated with fraktur-inspired ornaments and soft-sculpture heart-and-hands.

The heart-and-hand motif has appeared in American folk art since the 18th century. Symbolizing love and loyalty, it is seen often in Pennsylvania-German decoration. This contemporary heart-and-hand was stitched as a tree ornament.

that were made in the surrounding area. They also collect the work of contemporary craftspeople who carve and paint pieces in traditional Pennsylvania folk-art styles.

During the Christmas season, some of those pieces, such as handmade tree ornaments and carved crèche figures, are welcome additions to the trimmings. And there are always a few new decorations to surprise relatives when they return for the holiday. The small window tree in the living room (preceding overleaf), as well as the large tree in the dining room (see pages 126-127), for example, are decorated with contemporary fraktur ornaments, inspired by the illustrated manuscripts of the Pennsylvania Germans. *Continued*

*The folk-art rooster in the Christmas vignette above recalls the work of William Schimmel,*

*a 19th-century Pennsylvania carver.*

Topped by pine sprigs, the frames on the folk-art prints in the living room at left were crafted and grain-painted by the homeowners. The three-story dollhouse boasts its own tiny Christmas tree behind the miniature picket fence, as well as a pair of delightfully oversized stockings.

*Taufshein, or baptismal records, like the framed example above, were traditionally kept by Pennsylvania-German families. The Nativity figures displayed below the work were carved and painted by a contemporary craftsman.*

Caught up in the spirit of Christmas, the family always embrace the season's traditions wholeheartedly. Every niche and window ledge holds a reminder of the holiday. Greens and ribbons deck picture frames and mirrors. Even in the bedrooms, clusters of folk-art toys and greenery create a sense of nostalgic charm.

"Celebration is important and decorating is part of the enchantment, but it doesn't just happen," says one owner. "Preparations can be exhausting—particularly when it's two a.m. and the tree lights don't work—but it's worth it," she adds. "It's a gift to your family and friends."

*Folk-art toys sporting bright red ribbons add Christmas cheer to the bedroom at right.*

# SPRINGERLE

Springerle, anise-flavored cookies molded with decorative designs, are believed to have originated in Germany in the 17th or 18th century. The descendants of earlier molded cookies made from honey-sweetened dough or from marzipan, springerle were baked at holidays, and reached their height of popularity in the early 19th century.

The word *springerle,* from a southern German dialect, means to jump up, referring to the action of the dough, which doubles in height as the cookies bake. These extremely hard cookies were often decorated with colored-sugar mixtures, hung on a Christmas tree, and saved from year to year.

The making of springerle molds was an art in itself. The collection at left includes 19th-century examples as well as a new piece (with the large floral image).

The following recipe is adapted from a classic German-American springerle recipe published in 1856 by Wilhelm Vollmer in his *United States Cook Book.* To make sure your dough takes the sharpest design impression, you should use a true springerle mold or a springerle rolling pin and try pressing out a few cookies to perfect your technique.

## SPRINGERLE COOKIES

4 eggs
2 cups superfine sugar
Grated zest of ½ lemon

2½ teaspoons aniseed
About 5 cups flour
Olive oil

**1.** About 30 minutes before making dough, place springerle molds in refrigerator to chill (chilled molds will help prevent dough from sticking). As you work with one mold, keep others in refrigerator.

**2.** To make dough, in large bowl beat eggs to a thick froth. Sift in sugar gradually, and beat until creamy. Add lemon zest and aniseed, then gradually fold in 3½ cups of the flour. Depending on type of flour used and the weather, dough may be too sticky. If this is the case, lightly flour work surface and place dough on it. Using your hands, work an additional ½ to 1½ cups flour into dough, being careful to add only enough to keep dough from sticking to rolling pin when it is rolled out.

**3.** Brush chilled springerle molds very lightly with olive oil, then wipe molds with cloth. If images are elaborate, dust molds lightly with flour.

**4.** Lightly flour work surface. Divide dough into thirds and roll out to ½-inch thickness. One at a time, press each mold into dough and gently pull it away. Cut cookies out along borders (true springerle cookies always have raised borders). Place them on ungreased baking sheets to dry for at least 12 hours, enabling imprinted design to set. (Dry cookies in unheated room or cool part of house to prevent them from cracking during baking.) If you wish to use cookies as decorations, pierce them with skewer at this time; be sure hole is not too small or it will close during baking.

**5.** To bake, preheat oven to 325°. Remove cookies from ungreased baking sheets; lightly grease sheets. Replace cookies on greased baking sheets and bake for 15 to 20 minutes, or until bottoms are golden brown (tops will remain pale).

Makes 5 to 6 dozen 2-inch cookies

# A Texas Holiday

In central Texas, the winters are mild. "Even at Christmas time," says one of the owners of this 1870s farmhouse, "I can usually cut flowers in the garden for centerpieces, and we can still enjoy dining on the back porch—our favorite place to eat."

Used as a weekend home by a Houston couple and their three daughters, the house is situated on a 136-acre expanse of farmland. With its simple lines, it is typical of many farmhouses in central Texas built by German immigrants in the second half of the 19th century. The paneled and painted rooms are showcases for the couple's collection of Texas furnishings, also crafted by the German settlers; using hand tools and local woods such as longleaf pine and cypress, the

Continued

*A ten-foot table, above, is used for outdoor family dining about ten months out of the year. Decoys, cedar boughs, pinecones, and fruit make up the Christmas centerpiece.*

*Built by German settlers in the 1870s, this Texas farmhouse features a breezy front porch, opposite, with gingerbread trim typical of the period and region. A simple wreath decorates the door at holiday time.*

immigrants created vernacular furniture in the Biedermeier style then popular in their homeland. Because the furniture was made only from around 1840 to 1870, it is quite rare and is eagerly sought after today.

Complementing the furniture are the family's collections of antique toys and stars, which are continually rearranged throughout the house and which look particularly effective at Christmas. Red-and-white quilts and embroidered pillow shams also provide bright notes of color in keeping with the season. "I've never had the couches upholstered, the owner says, "because it's much more interesting to use different quilts as coverings instead."

Beginning in November, the women in the family cut grapevines in the yard and twine them into wreaths to hang in the house or to give as gifts. As the holiday approaches, they gather native cedar and yaupon (a type of holly with shiny green leaves and red berries) from the property and use the cuttings to decorate tables and mantelpieces. "I like to keep the decorations as they might have been when the original

*Continued*

*In the living room, candies are clustered in bowls, above, while vine wreaths hang by the fireplace at*

*right; on the mantle is an embroidered shelf trimming of the type used in pantries in 19th-century*

*German-American households. The message conveys the blessing "Compassion and Purity."*

*In the bedroom above, a holiday tree is decorated with children's playthings and handmade ornaments. The doll beds are antiques.*

settlers lived here," says one of the homeowners.

The small trees that are set up in the bedrooms have been cut to thin out the grove of cedars in the yard. Instead of using conventional ornaments on these unique Christmas trees, the owners opt for toys and textiles. On one, miniature dustpans, buckets, and chairs appear; another is trimmed with children's clothing and a small patchwork Christmas stocking. Because the family collections include antique cookie cutters, the annual round of Christmas baking usually produces several batches of cookie ornaments as well. Such improvised decorations only add to the old-fashioned warmth of the house.

*In the bedroom opposite, a mantel decked with holiday greenery becomes a festive showcase for the homeowners' collections of 19th-century papier-mâché horses and redware apple banks, which were made from about 1700 to the mid-1800s.*

# Garland Ideas

Creating Christmas garlands like those at right, which display some innovative twists on more familiar themes, can be as much fun for adults as it is for children. And making them is a simple matter of using ordinary materials in imaginative ways. Most of those shown here—beads, pretzels, macaroni, gumdrops, tiny bells, cork balls, and stick-on stars—are available at novelty stores and supermarkets. For the best results when making and storing garlands, consider the following tips:

◆ If you want to string materials on an "invisible" thread, use sturdy nylon or buttonhole thread.

◆ If you want your "string" to show, use colorful ribbons or thick, shiny cords.

◆ To string tiny pinecones, which are fragile, lay them on a tabletop and pierce them gently with a sharp sewing needle threaded with nylon or buttonhole thread.

◆ If you wish to spray-paint any of the materials—paint works particularly well on pasta and pinecones—be sure to do so before stringing them.

◆ To store your garlands tangle-free, carefully wind them around cardboard wrapping-paper tubes.

# Christmas
# in Santa Fe

O n Christmas Eve, the city of Santa Fe
and the surrounding countryside sparkle with thousands of *farolitos,* like
those in the courtyard of this New Mexico
residence. Placed along walls and paths, and on
the flat adobe roofs, these "little lanterns" (actually candles set in sand inside paper bags),
symbolically light the way for Joseph and Mary
in their search for shelter, and herald the arrival
of the Santo Niño, or Christ child.

This courtyard fronts a large house in a valley
just outside Santa Fe. Designed and built twelve
years ago by its present owners, the house recalls
the prevalent architectural style of the region—
low adobes traditionally built of clay or of bricks
made with sun-dried clay and straw—which
dates back to the 1600s. The residence is a home
to the couple and their three young sons; a sepa-
rate building serves as a pottery studio. Decorated with the handiwork of craftspeople from
Santa Fe and Mexico, the rooms are particularly
colorful at Christmas.

Like almost everything else in and around
Santa Fe, Christmas festivities are a mix of Indian, Hispanic, and Anglo-American customs.
Although the family celebrate with some conventional traditions, like decorating a tree and
hanging up stockings, their holiday menu is
apt to stray from the standard American fare to
include regional New Mexican specialties spiced
with red and green chilies. Dinner is usually
*Continued*

*Christmas in New Mexico is not Christmas without
the lighting of farolitos like those at left.*

*Favorites among the family's Christmas decorations are the Mexican tin ornaments above. Pieces like these are available in such shapes as birds, animals, and fish, as well as in more traditional Christmas designs like churches and trees. The shiny embossed tin creates a glittering effect when the ornament is hung on the tree.*

followed by a trip to a neighboring pueblo at Tesuque or San Ildefonso to view the seasonal rites of the Turtle Dance or the Evergreen Man. "In many ways," one homeowner says, "the Indian dances give true spirit to the holiday."

Another family tradition involves participation in an annual Christmas fair at which area residents and local craftspeople exchange ornaments of their own making. Many decorations on the family's tree, including cloth Navajo dolls, and small, clay Pueblo Indian figures, have come from the event. Most of the cloth and wooden toys displayed under the tree were also locally made. "On Christmas morning, however," one homeowner says, "the children are more apt to find more contemporary toys."  *Continued*

*Furnishings designed by one of the owners include the child-size and painted cupboards at right.*

Regional accents are also evident in the kitchen, which features traditional southwestern *vigas*, or heavy timbers, spanning the width of the ceiling, and a raised-hearth fireplace in which logs are burned vertically. Red-chili wreaths like those shown here are made throughout the year in Santa Fe, but are particularly popular as decorations at Christmas. Other decorations include Mexican tin and pottery candelabra, a group of Santa figures—including a Santa cat—made by a local craftsman, and stockings with the children's names and birth dates that were knit by an old family friend.

*Smoothly rounded with plaster, Santa Fe fireplaces are typically built into a corner or extended into a room, as in the kitchen, above. Decorated for Christmas, this fireplace also has an adjoining* banco, *or bench—the perfect spot for warming oneself on a chilly holiday evening.*

*Decorated pottery and tiles made by the homeowners are found in the kitchen, left.*

# THREE

# Setting the Christmas Table

*trimmings and traditions
for holiday meals*

Holiday entertaining—whether it involves an intimate family dinner or a large party for friends and neighbors—is an important part of Christmas. Such gatherings provide the opportunity to make and enjoy special recipes (including old favorites and creative new ones) and to add festive touches to the table.

While tradition is important, new twists and fresh ideas are welcome at these annual get-togethers. This chapter looks at the holiday tables, both casual and formal, in seven homes; the settings display distinctive approaches to entertaining for dinner, brunch, and even a children's holiday tea. You will also find a menu and recipes for a classic Christmas dinner—roast goose and all the accompaniments—that is both memorable and easy to prepare, as well as directions for a sparkling holiday centerpiece. Indeed, all the ingredients for an outstanding country Christmas are here.

*Fruit-shaped ornaments and variegated ivy make an unusual Christmas centerpiece.*

# A Colonial Celebration

*Wine is served, above, from the top of a 1690 Hadley chest. Holly and poinsettias are displayed in an English delft vase and bowl. The gentleman in the portrait is Colonel Samuel Clark, who purchased the house in 1788.*

Candlelight sets a warm tone for a holiday buffet in this Connecticut dining room where four generations of a family gather at Christmas. The table features a fruit pyramid, a type of centerpiece that first became popular in America around 1700. The capon is prepared in the colonial style: roasted in a reflector oven on the hearth. The rest of the dishes—including wild rice casserole, cranberry-pecan bread, apple torte, and rum cake—are made, says the homeowner, "simply because the family like them."

*Boxwood, holly, and apples were used to make the traditional fruit pyramid centerpiece at right.*

# Country-
# Store Feast

*Santas add a playful charm*
*to the dining area at right.*
*Each of the figures is hand-*
*made and no two are alike.*
*Dried pomegranates deco-*
*rate the garland draped*
*from the counter.*

This Chester County, Pennsylvania, dining area is the center of a great deal of entertaining at holiday time. On Christmas Eve the homeowners, their children, and their grandchildren get together here for a light dinner that is likely to feature shrimp and other hors d'oeuvres, soup, and a dessert such as chocolate fondue. A cranberry punch, which both the children and the adults can enjoy, is served from an antique yellowware bowl.

Around the room are a variety of Christmas decorations, including a group of wood, fabric, and cornhusk Santas, all made by contemporary craftspeople whose work the couple sell at their country store.

Housed in the same large stone 1759 building as the residence, the store provides an excuse for a second holiday party. At this occasion, friends and customers are invited to a "Candlelight Christmas" open house. The entire shop and house are lit solely by candles placed in the windows, on tabletops, and in chandeliers. Between 200 and 300 people come by to enjoy wassail and hot mulled cider, and to have a peek at the family Christmas tree decorated with old-fashioned handmade ornaments. "I knew the party was going well," one homeowner says, "when a girl came up to me and said, 'this place is like fairyland, it's exactly what Christmas should look like.'"

*Above, an antique yellowware bowl serves as a holiday centerpiece when surrounded by princess pine, fruit,*

*nuts, rose hips, and cinnamon sticks. The contemporary sgraffito plates are made by a Texas potter.*

# Christmas
# Romance

*Three different patterns of antique French porcelain are combined in the holiday place settings above. As a romantic touch, pink carnations and white pine are tied with ribbon to lace-edged linen napkins.*

The owners of this Massachusetts house do quite a bit of entertaining throughout the year, but Christmas dinner, they say, is reserved just for the immediate family.

For this occasion, they set an elegant Christmas table in the living room. A collector of American furniture and "almost everything that's pretty," one of the homeowners loves to decorate the table—a New York Federal-period piece—with some of her favorite treasures. A romantic holiday look is created by mixing tableware patterns that share the themes of lace, flowers, and pastel colors. The unusual pink-gold candlesticks and cornucopia vases are

Steuben art glass from the 1920s decorated with contrasting colored-glass vines and flowers, and filled with holiday sprays of white pine, cedar, and deep-pink roses. At each place setting, American swirled cranberry-glass goblets are paired with engraved crystal stemware.

The traditional Christmas dinner regularly includes an old family recipe for fresh cranberry frappé—a sherbetlike ice served in little glass cups—which accompanies the main dish of roast turkey or sliced tenderloin of beef. And among the special desserts that are offered each year is the family favorite—homemade pecan pie, with a dollop of whipped cream.

*Complementing the elegant table setting, the porcelain angels on the mantel at left are part of a collection of angel orchestras set out each Christmas.*

# SUGAR-GLAZED FRUIT

Sugar-glazed fruit shown off in a silver basket or in a porcelain bowl is one of the prettiest holiday table decorations you can make. It is also among the easiest: all you need are fruits, egg white, and granulated sugar.

Select fruits that vary in color and size, such as red, yellow, and green pears, peaches with a rosy blush, and several types of grapes. You may also want to include some exotic varieties, such as the angular starfruit in the arrangement at left. The fruits should be unbruised and firm, and not fully ripened, or they will turn soft in a day or two.

Make sure the fruits are dry and at room temperature. Pour granulated sugar onto a plate. Mix egg white lightly in a bowl, but do not let it become frothy. (You can judge by eye the quantity of egg white and sugar needed for the amount of fruit being used.) With a pastry brush, coat a piece of fruit with the egg white, roll it in the sugar, and place it on a cake rack to dry. Repeat the process until all the fruits are glazed. Let the fruits sit at room temperature for at least an hour before handling. (Keep in mind that because the egg white is raw and unrefrigerated, glazed fruit should never be eaten; it is a decoration only.) If you place the bowl of sugar-glazed fruit where it catches the light of candles or a chandelier, the sugar will sparkle.

Christmas Eve is the time traditionally reserved by the owners of this Victorian house for their holiday dinner. "On Christmas day," they explain, "it's too hard to get the children back to earth to do anything serious once they open their gifts."

The family's traditional dinner of soup, roast duck or guinea hens, and plum pudding with hard sauce is served in their dining room, which has been restored to period style with eleven different wallpaper patterns on the ceiling and walls. Many of the furnishings are heirlooms, but the couple have also found Victorian pieces, such as the sideboard, at auctions and shows.

At Christmas time, even the decorations in the room have a romantic, old-fashioned look. Garlands around the window and doorway are made with princess pine. Tiny white porcelain birds and red bows are tucked into the greens on the window ledge, and decorative hand-painted compotes are used for the arrangements of fruits and roses on the table and sideboard.

*The mirrored sideboard above provides a glimpse of the Christmas tree in the hall. Amaryllis blossoms are arranged in a glass vase, and lusterware is displayed on the shelf over the mirror.*

# Victorian Touches

*For Christmas dinner, an antique crocheted tablecloth from China is used over a red liner on the dining room table at left. The family like to make frequent use of their antique tableware, including this gold-and-red Limoges service.*

# Family Traditions

*Spode Christmas dinner-ware, above, is used each holiday season. The 19th-century silver napkin rings were collected one at a time. "Each is engraved with an old-fashioned name like Neddy or Herman," says one homeowner. "We all like discovering whose name we've got each year."*

When Christmas dinner is served in this Wisconsin house, it includes an element of surprise. A cranberry torte—an old family favorite that completes the meal—is baked with a penny in it; whoever finds the penny is assured luck for the coming year.

The family, in fact, celebrate Christmas with many unique dining and decorating traditions. The smoked turkey served at their table each year is prepared by the local blacksmith, who stops working at his forge long enough to operate his own smokehouse. And every year the owners showcase their collection of early glass and fabric Santa ornaments on the six-foot antique feather tree in a corner of the dining room. A painted child's sled, topped with a collection of 19th-century toy sheep and a Santa figure crafted by a family friend, makes an unusual centerpiece.

At left, an 18th-century
American swing-leg cherry
dining table is set for Christmas dinner. The Norwegian
table runner, woven in a
reindeer pattern, and the
Irish crystal goblets represent two branches of
the family tree.

125

# A Christmas Tea

Children love to have their own grown-up parties: this Pennsylvania dining room is the setting for a child-size Christmas tea. Although the tree is decorated for the entire family's enjoyment, its painted fraktur ornaments and gingham hearts are particularly appealing to children.

On the table, the menagerie centerpiece was assembled from a collection of contemporary folk art. An antique Gaudy Welsh tea service will be used to serve cocoa, and spatterware plates are soon to be filled with sandwiches, Christmas cookies, and a taste of fruitcake made from a hundred-year-old family recipe.

*Part of the centerpiece for a children's Christmas tea party, the little wooden house above is actually an antique sewing box; the hinged roof opens. The plates, cups, and saucers are contemporary spatterware.*

*On the side table at left sits a contemporary bird tree, a traditional form of Pennsylvania folk art.*

# New Mexico Flavor

*The rabbit plate above is from a special line of Christmas pottery made by the homeowners. Clustered in the centerpiece are a doll-size tea set and bowls, and a miniature black-and-white Acoma Indian pottery jar.*

Tucked into a nook under the stairs, the table in this New Mexico kitchen is laid out for a casual Christmas brunch; the blue-painted *banco*, built along the walls, provides plenty of seating. Strings of red-chili Christmas lights and a cluster of Mexican clay villagers in the window enliven the room.

The table is set with rabbit-motif plates that were made and decorated by the homeowners (who work together as potters) and with chunky blue and gold blown-glass goblets. Fruit, pine boughs, and ceramic Nativity figures from Oaxaca make up the centerpiece.

When brunch is presented, the menu is apt to include regional favorites. "Making tamales is always a special event," one family member says, "because we make them from scratch and it takes all day." Blue-corn tortillas—prepared from cornmeal blue-black in color—are also served, as is Chili Colorado, which includes, appropriately, both red and green chilies.

A sunny corner of the kitchen
is a comfortable spot for a
casual holiday brunch. Much
of the artwork that appears
in the room, such as the folk-
art snake and Rio Grande
painting, was made by
family members.

# A HOLIDAY BUFFET

Perfect for Christmas or New Year's, the buffet menu offered below (with recipes continuing on the following pages) features a fragrant roast goose with wild rice-chestnut stuffing, along with sautéed vegetables and a festive fruit tart that is delicious served with ice cream. Oysters on the half shell make an elegant starter for the meal and cranberry relish and biscuits complement the main dishes.

While this meal is easy to prepare—the goose is only slightly more complicated to roast than a turkey and the tart dough is made in a food processor—it does require time. The stuffing takes about an hour to make, then the goose roasts for a little over four hours and sits for another thirty minutes before carving.

Don't forget to leave time to set an attractive table. Here, green-stemmed goblets and a crystal compote filled with colorful Christmas ornaments add a holiday touch.

---

· MENU ·

*Oysters on the Half Shell*

*Roast Goose with Wild Rice-Chestnut Stuffing*

*Mélange of Vegetables with Tarragon Butter*

*Cranberry Relish · Country Biscuits*

*Cranberry-Apple Tart with Walnut Crust*

*Vanilla Ice Cream · Spiced Coffee*

*Champagne*

◆

## ROAST GOOSE WITH WILD RICE-CHESTNUT STUFFING

| | |
|---|---|
| 1 goose, about 14 pounds, giblets and neck trimmed and reserved | 1½ cups canned chicken broth |
| 1 teaspoon salt | 1 small onion |
| 1 teaspoon pepper | 12 juniper berries, crushed |
| Wild Rice-Chestnut Stuffing (see next page) | 1 bay leaf |
| | 1 cup water |
| | 3 tablespoons flour |

**1.** Preheat oven to 400°. Cut off and discard excess fat from cavity of goose. Rinse and dry goose and sprinkle cavity with salt and pepper. Loosely stuff goose with about 10 cups Wild Rice-Chestnut Stuffing, then truss opening with skewers and string. Place remaining stuffing in greased baking dish and cover with foil; set aside.

**2.** Prick skin of goose all over with fork to allow excess fat to drip off during cooking. Place goose, breast-side up, on rack in deep roasting pan, and roast for 20 minutes.

**3.** Reduce oven temperature to 325°, cover goose loosely with foil, and roast for an additional 17 minutes per pound (about 4 hours and 20 minutes total for a 14-pound goose). Remove foil after 2 hours. Using basting bulb or cooking spoon, periodically remove fat from roasting pan, leaving cooking juices in pan. Carefully pour hot fat (there may be as much as 1 quart) into large can or foil pan to cool and solidify before discarding it. Goose is done when skin is browned, drumstick moves easily in its socket, and juices run clear when goose is pierced with a sharp knife; internal temperature should register 180°.

**4.** While goose cooks, in small saucepan bring giblets and neck, chicken broth, whole onion, juniper berries, bay leaf, and water to a boil over medium-high heat. Cover pan tightly, reduce heat to low, and simmer gently for about 1 hour. Strain broth, reserving giblets and neck; discard other solids. Remove meat from neck and chop neck meat and giblets. Set aside broth and chopped neck meat and giblets.

**5.** One hour before goose is done, place reserved dish of stuffing in oven.

**6.** When goose is cooked, transfer to carving board and cover loosely with foil; let rest for 30 minutes before carving.

**7.** To make gravy, reheat giblet broth over low heat. Pour off all but ¼ cup of liquid from roasting pan. Place roasting-pan over medium heat and slowly stir in flour. Cook, stirring frequently, until flour is lightly browned, about 1 minute.

**8.** Add reheated broth and reserved chopped neck meat and giblets, stirring constantly. Simmer gravy until it has thickened and lost any taste of uncooked flour, 5 to 7 minutes. Stir to blend thoroughly; season with additional salt and pepper, if desired. Keep gravy warm over very low heat while you carve the goose. 8 servings

◆

## WILD RICE-CHESTNUT STUFFING

4 cups canned chicken broth
1 cup raw wild rice, rinsed
1 cup raw brown rice
2 tablespoons butter
2 tablespoons olive oil
3 medium-size leeks (white part
    only), washed and coarsely
    chopped (about 1 pound),
    or 4 cups chopped onions
1 pound country-style sausage,
    casings removed

½ pound fresh mushrooms,
    coarsely chopped
1 can (10 ounces) chestnuts packed
    in water, drained, or 35 whole
    chestnuts, cooked, shelled,
    and halved
2 cups diced carrots
½ cup chopped parsley
2 teaspoons crumbled sage
½ teaspoon pepper

**1.** In medium-size saucepan, bring broth to a boil over medium-high heat. Stir in wild rice and brown rice, cover pan, reduce heat to medium-low, and simmer until rices are tender and most of liquid is absorbed, 35 to 40 minutes. Remove pan from heat; set aside.

**2.** In large skillet, melt butter in oil over medium-high heat. Add leeks and sauté until they are well coated with butter, 1 to 2 minutes.

**3.** Add sausage, breaking it up with a spoon. Add mushrooms and cook until sausage is no longer pink, 5 to 10 minutes. Remove skillet from heat.

**4.** Stir in cooked rice, chestnuts, carrots, parsley, sage, and pepper. Let stuffing cool slightly before using. Makes about 16 cups

To make your buffet table especially festive, tie glittery ribbons around napkins and silverware. For convenience, place the napkins and silver in a basket, as above, or in individual tall glasses.

## MELANGE OF VEGETABLES WITH TARRAGON BUTTER

2 tablespoons butter
2 tablespoons olive oil
1 red onion, thinly sliced
2 cloves garlic, crushed through
   a press
4 cups broccoli florets
2 large red bell peppers, slivered
   (about 2 cups)

2 large yellow or green bell
   peppers, slivered (about 2 cups)
1 tablespoon chopped fresh
   tarragon, or ½ teaspoon dried
½ teaspoon salt
¼ teaspoon pepper
1 cup walnut halves

**1.** In large skillet, melt butter in oil over medium-high heat. Add onion and garlic, and cook, stirring, until onion begins to wilt, 1 to 2 minutes.

**2.** Add broccoli and bell peppers, and cook, stirring, until vegetables are just tender, 5 to 7 minutes.

**3.** Stir in tarragon, salt, and pepper, then sprinkle walnuts over vegetables. Serve immediately.                     8 servings

◆

## CRANBERRY-APPLE TART WITH WALNUT CRUST

**Pastry**
⅔ cup chopped walnuts
1 cup flour
2 tablespoons sugar
¼ teaspoon salt
⅓ cup chilled butter, cut into
   pieces
2 to 3 tablespoons ice water

**Filling**
3 Granny Smith apples (about
   1 pound), peeled and sliced
   ¼ inch thick
2 tablespoons flour
⅓ cup plus 2 tablespoons sugar
2 teaspoons grated orange zest
1 cup fresh or frozen cranberries
¼ cup orange juice
1 teaspoon cornstarch

Spiced coffee is a pleasing end to a holiday dinner. To prepare it, in a mug stir together 1 tablespoon each maple syrup and heavy cream. Add a pinch each of ground cloves and ginger, and fill the mug with hot coffee. Stir again and let stand 1 to 2 minutes. Garnish the mug with an orange slice or cinnamon stick, and top the coffee with a dollop of whipped cream, if desired.

**1.** Make the pastry: In food processor, process walnuts, pulsing machine on and off until walnuts are coarsely ground. Add flour, sugar, and salt, and pulse just until mixed, 2 to 3 seconds. Add butter and pulse until mixture resembles coarse cornmeal, 5 to 10 seconds. With processor running, add just enough ice water to form a cohesive dough. Remove dough from processor, form into a ball, flatten into a disk, and wrap in plastic wrap. Refrigerate for at least 30 minutes, or until well chilled.

**2.** Meanwhile, in large bowl, toss apples with flour, 2 tablespoons of the sugar, and 1 teaspoon of the orange zest; set aside.

**3.** Preheat oven to 375°.

**4.** Roll dough into an 11-inch circle and fit it into a 9-inch tart pan with removable bottom. Trim overhang. Fill pastry with apple mixture. Bake for 25 minutes.

**5.** Meanwhile, in small saucepan, combine cranberries, remaining ⅓ cup sugar and 1 teaspoon orange zest, orange juice, and cornstarch, and stir to dissolve cornstarch and sugar. Cook over medium heat, stirring constantly, until mixture comes to a boil and thickens, about 5 minutes. Remove pan from heat.

**6.** When tart has baked for 25 minutes, spoon cranberry mixture evenly over apples and bake for another 10 minutes, or until crust is golden and apples are tender.

**7.** Transfer tart to rack to cool for 15 minutes before removing sides of pan. Leave tart on pan bottom to serve.             Makes one 9-inch tart

134

# Christmas Collectibles

*ornaments, cards, stockings,
and other mementos
of the season*

Christmas collectibles like those shown on the following pages, including vintage tree trimmings, greeting cards, candy boxes, puzzles, and games, are fascinating reminders of a decorating tradition that did not take firm root in America until the 1800s. Manufacturers began making ornaments widely available around 1870, and introduced light bulbs around 1900, opening a new world of possibilities for trimming the tree. While Japanese and American firms were responsible for a host of lights and tree decorations, European countries—particularly Germany—produced a large proportion of the Christmas collectibles sought after today.

The character of Santa Claus, along with a cast of other gift-bearers in their many guises, has also captured the imaginations of collectors, as have 19th-century greeting cards like those printed by Louis Prang, the first manufacturer of Christmas cards in America. Such vintage mementos, as well as books and ephemera, are a good place for the new collector to start.

*Vintage tree bulbs, made in Japan, depict Santa Claus in varied forms.*

# Glass Ornaments

*Among the hand-blown globe- and teardrop-shaped German-made kugels above, the amethyst-colored piece is the rarest. While most kugels are fitted with a brass cap, some examples feature an elongated "pike" at the top into which a cork with a metal loop hanger would be fitted.*

Glass ornaments were among the first decorations made for the Christmas tree. One of the initial types was the *kugel* (meaning "ball"), which originated in the first part of the 1800s in the small glassmaking center of Lauscha, Germany. Early kugels were hung on the holiday trees of the craftsmen who made them, and were gradually discovered by other Christmas-loving Germans. The first written record of kugels being produced as ornaments appears in 1848, with an order for "six dozen Christmas tree ornaments in three sizes" recorded in a Lauscha glass blower's ledger.

*Continued*

*The early-20th-century German molded figural ornaments at right include a rare bust of Uncle Sam and several uncommon religious ornaments.*

*Made in Germany around 1900, delicate glass ornaments like those above—decorated with cotton batting, cardboard, printed paper, and crinkled wire—reflect the Victorian fascination with the idea of flight. Because adding the wire wrapping was a painstaking task, it was often left to a patient grandmother in the ornament maker's family.*

Free-blown over open fires and silvered with lead or zinc, kugels were made not only in the shape of a ball but also in teardrop and oval shapes. The irregular heat of the open fire gave these pieces the relatively thick walls that are the distinguishing feature of true kugels, and it is because of these thick walls that many of the ornaments survive today. Sizes range from one to four inches in diameter, and the most common colors are cobalt, green, silver, gold, red, and amethyst.

While kugels continued to be free-blown over fires for many years, by 1867 an adjustable gas burner had been invented, enabling craftsmen to blow more delicate, thin-walled balls (sometimes mistakenly called kugels). About the same time, molded figural ornaments also originated in the town of Lauscha, supposedly after an inventive craftsman experimented by blowing molten glass into a cookie mold.

The earliest molded pieces were shaped like pinecones, fruits, or icicles, but between the 1890s and 1930s some five thousand different designs, including fruits and vegetables, animals, birds, buildings, vehicles, Santas, and other human and storybook figures, were made. These molded pieces were often decorated—with lacquer, paint, glitter, paper scrap, or crinkled wire. Most were fitted with a wire loop for hanging; other, rarer examples had a metal clip at the base.

Around 1880, F. W. Woolworth began importing all of these glass ornaments. His imports dominated the market until 1939 when, urged by Woolworth, Corning Glass Works produced the first American machine-made glass balls.

*The Santas, birds, comic figures, and buildings opposite, made between 1900 and the 1930s, are just some of the thousands of molded ornament designs produced by German glass blowers.*

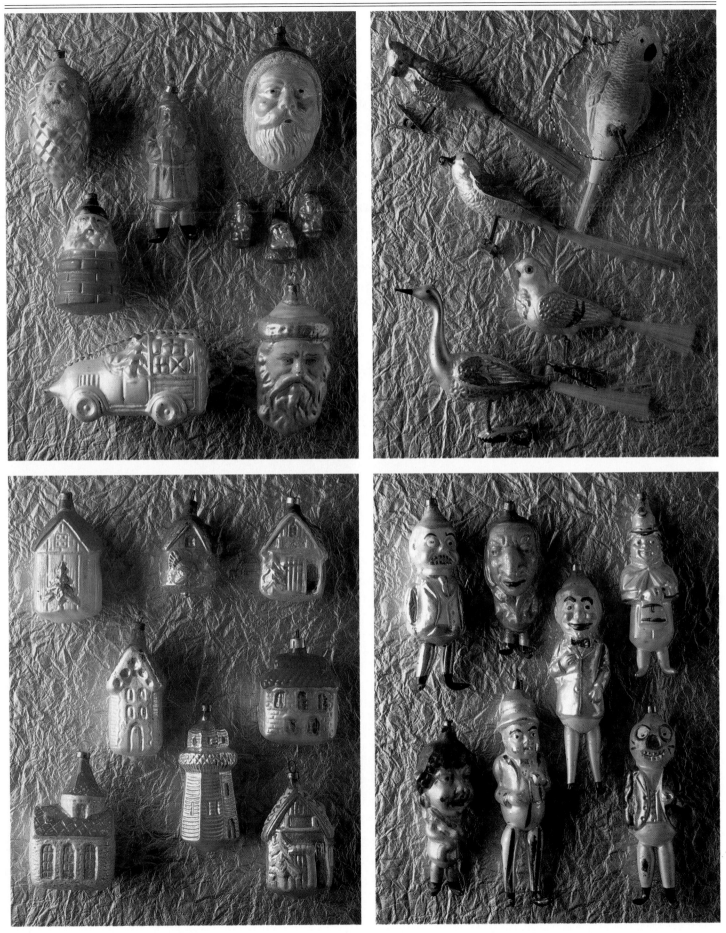

# Wax and Sebnitz Ornaments

The rare German Sebnitz ornaments at right, dating from 1870 to 1915, were made by wrapping crinkled wire and punched metal around cotton. One of the most common themes for Sebnitz ornaments was transportation, and many variations on carriages and airships exist. Pieces that include wax figures are particularly prized by collectors.

German-made wax Christmas ornaments, much sought after by collectors, were particularly popular in America from the late 1800s until about 1930. Some of the earliest wax pieces were tiny replicas of the Christ child, which might be wrapped in silk bunting or be placed in a nutshell "manger." Later forms included cherubim and angels complete with cardboard, plaster, or spun-glass wings, gauze sashes, and wire halos, as well as children, fruits, and animals.

Such wax figures were also incorporated into what have become known as Sebnitz ornaments—"combination" pieces of fabric, glass, paper, and metal, which were produced in Sebnitz, Germany, from 1870 until World War I. A Sebnitz ornament is distinguished by its unusual wrapping of metal foil punched with tiny holes. Rarely found in this country today, Sebnitz ornaments were generally made by cottage workers. Favorite forms included various means of transportation, animals, and babes in cradles.

*Made in Germany in the late 19th and early 20th centuries, the wax ornaments above are trimmed with gilded cardboard, spun glass, fabric, and ribbon. Most angels "flew" horizontally by means of a hook fixed on their backs, and some once held tiny tin or lead trumpets in their raised hands.*

# Dresden
# Ornaments

Characterized by their delicate construction and painstaking detail, so-called Dresden ornaments are considered to be among the most beautiful Christmas tree decorations ever produced. Made primarily in and around Dresden and Leipzig, Germany, between 1880 and 1914, these ornaments appear at first glance to have been wrought from precious metals but are actually constructed from carefully die-cut and embossed cardboard that has been decorated with some combination of gilding, silvering, and painting.

While Dresdens were fashioned in nearly every conceivable shape, common categories were animals, forms of transportation, musical instruments, and household articles. Some Dresdens are flat and are decorated on only one side, while others are "double," or made in mirror image so

*Continued*

*The cardboard Dresden ornaments above and at right, ranging from two to six inches in length, are prized for their fine workmanship and minute detailing.*

*Flat Dresden ornaments like those at right were often cut from gold-faced cardboard and painted on the back so that they would still look pretty as they twirled on the tree. In Victorian times such ornaments were not only hung on the Christmas tree, but also pasted into scrapbooks.*

the ornament looks the same from either side. The most intricate Dresdens, however, were three-dimensional miniatures, assembled from many tiny pieces.

The great detailing that distinguishes Dresden ornaments is the result of a process in which the cardboard is stamped between two metal dies engraved with the identical design in opposing relief. Even the most minute details, such as the individual needles on an evergreen bough or the leathery wrinkles on an elephant's trunk, were easily transferred from the dies to the thin, pliable paper stock. After the cardboard pieces were embossed and die-cut in a factory, cottage workers would assemble the ornaments and apply finishing touches such as bead eyes, upholstered coach seats, silk reins, and billowy puffs of cotton "smoke."

# CARE OF ORNAMENTS

Fragile Christmas ornaments, both new and antique, need special care to keep them in good condition from year to year. Blown-glass balls, embossed cardboard figures, and printed-paper "scraps," among other ornament types, all require delicate handling when being hung and put away for storage.

Since most ornaments are displayed on the tree during the holidays, it is important to be sure that your tree is secured tightly in its stand and cannot tip. Cushioning should also be placed under the tree to protect any ornament that does accidentally drop: a blanket, cotton pad, or foam sheet—at least as wide as the tree—is best. You can then simply cover the padding with a decorative tree skirt.

Before hanging an ornament, you should check that each cap, loop, or other attachment is secure. If you use thin wire hooks, bend them around a branch to prevent them from slipping. For extra protection, you can tie the top of the hook to the branch. The most delicate ornaments, which should be hung last, are best placed toward the middle or at the top of the tree, where they are less likely to be dislodged.

When the holidays are over, fragile ornaments should be individually wrapped and boxed for storage. One method is to pack each ornament in its own small box, layered between wads of paper, or wrapped in plastic "bubble pack," tissue, or newsprint. Another method is to store each ornament inside a plastic zip-locked bag; by leaving a little air in the bag when sealing it, you will provide a cushion for the ornament. (Avoid blowing into the bag, which creates damaging moisture.)

After you have wrapped the ornaments, place them in containers that are sturdy enough to withstand an accidental fall. There are cardboard boxes specially designed for ornament storage, featuring individual pockets that create a nest for each piece. Lidded plastic sweater boxes are also a good choice.

Keep the boxed ornaments in a cool, dry, ventilated place where they will not be exposed to moisture, mildew, direct sunlight, or extreme fluctuations in temperature. (Often basements are too damp and attics too hot.) Wherever you store the ornaments, secure the box so that it cannot fall, and be sure that nothing heavy can fall on it.

# Cotton
# Ornaments

*Spun-cotton ornaments like
the late-19th- and early-
20th-century German
examples at right were
favorites with children;
parents often hung these
inexpensive pieces on the
lowest tree branches so
that they could be touched
and played with. As a
consequence, antique cotton
ornaments in good condition
are hard to find.*

Around the turn of the century, German-made cotton ornaments—of spun cotton, cotton batting, and cotton wool—were nearly as popular as glass ornaments. A 1901 catalog listed thirty different cotton ornament designs—among them "Christmas Angels," "a chambermaid in a bright dress," and "a stork nest with three storks"—and American ladies' magazines of the period instructed readers on how to create their own cotton ornaments at home. In the 1920s, Japanese craftsmen entered the Christmas market, producing a wide variety of cotton ornaments less finely detailed than those from Germany.

The ornaments shown here are known as spun-cotton ornaments. They were fabricated by a process in which cotton and cellulose fibers were wound together around a wire or cardboard form. A layer of glue was then spread on the surface to add strength and provide a smooth base for the application of glitter, paint, and other decoration. Such ornaments are consequently distinguished by a hard "shell" that bears very little resemblance to natural cotton.

Among the most popular spun-cotton ornaments were those shaped like animals, fruits, vegetables, and people. Elaborate people ornaments were often detailed with printed-paper or composition faces, cardboard or crepe paper clothing, feathers, and ribbons. Fruit and vegetable ornaments, many with decorative stems and leaves, were realistically painted.

*The painted spun-cotton fruits and vegetables above, from Germany and Japan, are enhanced with naturalistic stems and leaves of wire, feathers, paper, and fabric.*

# Scrap Ornaments

In the mid-19th century, chromolithography—a process for mass-producing multicolor prints—was perfected in Germany, making reasonably priced color pictures available for the first time. Soon, Europeans and Americans alike were avidly collecting these pictures for their scrapbooks (a craze that would reach its peak during the latter half of the century). Consequently, chromolithographed images came to be known as scraps.

From about 1870 until the early 1900s, countless chromolithographed images were produced in Germany for use as holiday decorations. Imported and sold at stationery, book, and general stores, scraps could be purchased by the piece or in sheets—for creating homemade ornaments—or already fashioned into decorations.

The simplest type of scrap ornament is a complete silhouetted image—most commonly a Santa figure, an angel, a snowman, or a Christmas tree. Some of these hand- or die-cut ornaments were printed on only one side, while others might display a different image on each side, or two mirror images back-to-back. Many of these ornaments were decorated with mica glitter or strands of tinsel rope.

Other scrap ornaments incorporated the color pictures as only one element in an elaborate assemblage. A printed face or a half-figure, for example, might be "fleshed out" with cotton batting, crepe paper, or spun-glass clothing. And scrap scenes—which often included children, Santas, or cherubim—were frequently used to make a colorful central medallion for cotton batting stars, crosses, and rosettes.

Chromolithograph, or "scrap," ornaments like those opposite and at left were made between about 1880 and 1920 using images printed in Germany. Some of the ornaments, such as the angels with the fancy spun-glass skirt and the Lady Liberty with the star-sprinkled gown, were commercially produced. Others were probably homemade using scrap and bits of cotton batting, tinsel rope, cardboard, and paper.

# Figural Christmas Lights

*America was a major market for European figural Christmas bulbs like those at right, made in the early 1900s. While most collectors simply display them, some have adapted these screw-in bulbs to the type of Christmas tree wiring used today.*

A long with ornaments, candles were standard on the American Christmas tree until electric lights began to replace them in 1882. Pear-shaped and round bulbs were all that was available in this country until the early 1900s, when the Kremenetzky Electric Company of Vienna began exporting the first figural light bulbs. Hand-blown from clear glass in such shapes as fruits, flowers, animals, and Santas, figural bulbs were notable for their delicacy and beautiful hand-painted detailing.

Fine figural lights were also imported from Germany and Hungary, and around 1915 Japanese craftsmen began producing figural bulbs, primarily using translucent milk glass rather than clear glass because they found it held paint better and hid the filament if the paint wore off. Among the Japanese figural lights popular with Americans were cartoon figures like Popeye, Little Orphan Annie, and Dick Tracy.

*Unlike European bulbs, the Japanese bulbs above, made in the 1920s and 1930s, are threaded at the top. While most of these are milk glass, the game die is clear glass that has been painted.*

# Santa Figures

*Dating to the late 19th century, the figures at right are gift-bearers derived from Saint Nicholas, a 4th-century bishop (shown with staff and miter at center). Not all are kindly: those carrying switches, like the German Knecht Rupprecht in the green cloak (far right), are alter egos of the saint, meant to frighten bad children. The figure dressed in red has dropped a naughty child into his pack.*

The jolly, red-suited Santa Claus of modern Christmas lore is a composite of many folk figures—some benevolent and others surprisingly stern and forbidding. Over the years, the gift-bearer in his various incarnations has been reproduced in a number of forms, including a wide range of figures, some of which were used as ornaments, toys, and candy containers.

Many Santa pieces were made by German toymakers between 1860 and World War II, but some were also produced in 20th-century America and Japan. Figures ranging in height from a few inches to several feet can be found in chalkware, papier-mâché, wood, cardboard, or composition, and might be decorated with paint, fabric, fur, mica glitter, or cotton batting.

Most Santa characters are related to Saint

*Continued*

*The composition and papier-mâché Belsnickels opposite were made in Germany and range in size from 2½ to 24 inches. The larger figures are the scarcest.*

*Crafted mainly in Germany, the figures above depict Santa as the kindly present-bearer we imagine him as today. The jack-in-the-box is a rare and desirable piece.*

Nicholas, a legendary bishop who lived in Asia Minor in the 4th century. Known for his generous deeds in life, Nicholas was immortalized as the patron saint of children, who brought them gifts on December 5, the eve of his feast day. The charitable Nicholas was supposedly accompanied by a grotesque helper who punished the bad with coal and switches. This alter ego was variously known as Knecht Rupprecht (Servant Ruppert), Ru Klas (Rough Nicholas), or Pelz-Nikolaus (Fur-clad Nicholas), among other personas. Pelz-Nikolaus emigrated to America with German settlers and became known as Belsnickel. Today Belsnickel figures made in Germany between the 1870s and 1920 (and occasionally in America) are particularly popular

with Santa collectors. These gnomish, bearded figures carry evergreen sprigs or switches in their arms and are dressed in hooded cloaks.

With the Protestant Reformation in the 16th century, which forbade worship of saints, Nicholas took on a secular aspect: in England he became Father Christmas, for example, and in Germany, Weihnachtsmann (Christmas man). It is this secular Nicholas that is the basis for today's Santa, who, as Sinterklaas, came to America with the Dutch in 1624. Several literary works, including Clement Moore's 1822 poem "A Visit from St. Nicholas," helped transform the thin European saint into the rotund elf in fur-trimmed suit and cap we now envision as Santa Claus.

# THOMAS NAST'S CHRISTMAS

"A Visit from St. Nicholas," 1863-1864

Without Thomas Nast, our vision of Santa Claus might be very different. A political cartoonist who originated the familiar symbols of the Republican elephant and the Democratic donkey, Nast is thought to have been the first artist to draw Santa Claus as the "jolly old elf" we know today.

Nast was born in Germany in 1840 and emigrated to New York with his family at age six. As a teenager he enrolled in art school and, at fifteen, began his career as an illustrator. After jobs with several periodicals, he joined *Harper's Weekly* in 1862 as a war correspondent and began to produce acclaimed cartoons and Civil War sketches.

About the same time, Nast "met" Santa when a publisher asked him to illustrate a book of holiday poems that included Clement Moore's "A Visit from St. Nicholas." Combining imagery from Moore's verse, and his childhood memories of Christmas, Nast created a rotund, bearded, pipe-smoking figure in a wooly suit and cap, carrying a large sack of toys (see top row, left).

Nast's first Santa for *Harper's* appeared on January 3, 1863. Santa was shown visiting a Union camp and wearing a suit of stars and stripes (the artist was a staunch Union sympathizer). His next Santa for the magazine, published December 26, 1863, was part of a composite picture that included a soldier home on furlough.

Nast's Christmas illustrations for *Harper's* were so popular that each year for the next twenty-three years the artist would take time from cartooning to contribute holiday drawings to the magazine. At right are just some of those drawings, including the last one Nast did for *Harper's* (bottom row, right). It was published December 28, 1886, and fittingly illustrates a line from Moore's poem.

"Merry Christmas," January 4, 1879

"Caught!" December 24, 1881

"Christmas Post," January 4, 1879

"Merry Old Santa Claus," January 1, 1881

"Not a creature was stirring," December 28, 1886

# Candy Containers

<ittle containers designed especially to hold sweets (and occasionally a suitor's engagement ring) were popular as Christmas tree ornaments, tabletop decorations, and party favors between the 1870s and 1930s. Produced commercially on three continents—in Europe, America, and Asia—candy boxes were constructed primarily of foil, painted and embossed cardboard, scrap, papier-mâché, and crepe paper. These containers were fashioned in thousands of shapes, from simple suitcases, hatboxes, stockings, and cornucopias to elaborate-

*The candy containers at left were manufactured between the 1880s and 1920s for use as tree ornaments and party favors. The tiniest boxes, like the miniature Steinway grand piano shown here, could hold only one or two treats—a gumdrop, perhaps, or a couple of nuts. Today such candy boxes are hard to find because many were discarded after the contents were eaten.*

ly detailed grand pianos, guitars, and mandolins.

While most of these candy containers were made like boxes—with removable tops—others were designed to cleverly conceal their treasures. Papier-mâché containers shaped like carp (a delicacy on German Christmas tables) hid their contents behind "trap doors" molded into the scales. Shoes might be fitted with drawstring fabric pouches to hold the candy. And colorful paper rolls, called crackers, had to be tugged apart to yield their treats, thereby producing a loud—and startling—pop.

# Christmas Postcards

Christmas postcards were an offshoot of the trend for exchanging holiday greetings that began in the mid-1800s. Particularly popular in America in the early 1900s, these inexpensive pictorial cards were imported from Germany and England, and were also printed domestically.

Some of the most common designs included winter scenes, decorated trees, angels, children, and, of course, Santa Claus, a favorite among collectors today. Usually printed in full color, Christmas postcards might also be embossed and decorated with tinsel, silk fringe, or paper.

Novelty Christmas postcards were especially prized. One type was the hold-to-light card, on which certain details, like candles, stars, or Santa's buttons, were cut out and backed with translucent colored paper. When the card was held to a light, the cutouts glowed. Similar to these was the transparency card, a sort of "paper sandwich" in a cardboard frame: the scene printed on the thin top sheet was visible in daylight; another image, printed on the backing sheet, appeared only when the card was held to a light.

*Designed to be held up to a light, the novelty postcards above are shown unlit (top row) and transformed by the light (bottom row). The card of four dancing children, who encircle Saint Nick when he magically appears, is called a transparency. The others are hold-to-lights.*

*Many of the early-1900s Christmas postcards opposite show scenes of Santa on his yearly visit, a favorite subject. One particularly unusual card has a torso and legs of paper honeycomb.*

161

# CARDS BY LOUIS PRANG

The custom of exchanging Christmas cards was already established by the time Louis Prang produced his first cards in the early 1870s. But it was the German-immigrant printer who was responsible for bringing fine-art standards to this commercial commodity and for popularizing greeting cards in America.

Prang arrived in this country in 1850 at age twenty-six. In 1860, he opened his own chromolithography shop, L. Prang & Co., near Boston, where he specialized in quality art reproductions, maps, and trade cards. After an associate suggested that his floral-decorated business cards would also make appealing Christmas greetings, Prang printed his first cards for the English market in 1874. Their immediate acceptance led Prang to sell his cards the next year in America, where only European cards had been available.

Early Prang cards measured about 2 by 3½ inches and were printed with an image and a brief message on one side. During the next twenty years, his cards increased in size to 7 by 10 inches, carried longer verse, and were printed on both sides. Common motifs included flowers, birds, winter scenes, and angels.

Regardless of size or subject, all of Prang's cards displayed the technical excellence he demanded. They were printed using from eight to twenty color plates, and often featured black or red backgrounds to enhance the

designs. While Prang deemed lace, mechanical tricks, and other novelties vulgar, he did permit silk fringe and tassels.

To ensure the quality of his cards, Prang initiated an annual Christmas card design competition in 1880. Judged by leading artists, architects, and designers, the prestigious contest eventually offered prizes of up to $2,000. Not only did Prang publish cards with winning works by such well-known contemporary artists as

Thomas Moran and Elihu Vedder, he used losing entries, too.

Although Prang's cards were costlier than his competitors'—they were priced up to $1—they were more popular; the company printed nearly five million cards annually. By the late 1800s, however, inexpensive European Christmas postcards had eroded Prang's business. Rather than lower his prices by lowering his standards, he turned his presses to educational book printing in 1897.

The Christmas cards pictured on these two pages are examples of the exquisitely lithographed greetings produced by the printer Louis Prang, often called the father of the American Christmas card. The artwork for all of these cards was taken from winning entries in the Christmas card design competitions Prang held between 1880 and 1884. These high-profile contests were meant to increase both the popularity of the Christmas card and the public's appreciation of fine art.

# Toys and Games

The Christmas games at right are examples of just a few of the holiday toys made in the late 19th and early 20th centuries by such noted American firms as Parker Brothers, Milton Bradley, and McLoughlin Brothers. To save money, some companies would simply graft holiday art onto a generic game sold during the rest of the year.

Using chromolithography, both European and American toy firms and printers turned out colorful, graphic Christmas toys and games from about 1880 until approximately 1920. Because they were meant only for holiday amusement, these Christmas playthings were seldom produced in quantity and are rare today.

Among the most popular were board games, which generally involved a race across the board to a goal—a natural situation for the globe-trotting Santa Claus. In "The Game of Kriss Kringle's Visits," shown opposite, for example, each player tries to get all of Santa's presents as quickly as possible.

Christmas blocks (also called cubes) and jigsaw puzzles, above, were often made by the same companies that produced children's picture books. The images from the books were simply cut into squares that could be glued onto the blocks, or were mounted on cardboard and cut into interlocking pieces for a puzzle.

*Christmas picture puzzles and blocks like those above are valued not only for their beautiful graphics but also because all the pieces have remained intact.*

# Christmas Stockings

The custom of hanging stockings by the fireplace on Christmas Eve can be traced to a Saint Nicholas legend. To help an impoverished nobleman provide dowries for his daughters, the generous Saint Nick threw gold coins down the chimney. The coins magically landed in stockings hung by the fire to dry. In America, those hoping for a sampling of Saint Nick's beneficence began hanging stockings—either from the mantel, staircase, or tree—in the early 1800s.

The first stockings were no more than or-

*Hung by the chimney with care, the vintage stockings at left range from simple everyday hose to the fancy printed types popular from the 1890s to the 1930s. The patchwork stocking is homemade from flannel and twill scraps. The three brick-patterned stockings bear holiday sayings, including a quote from Clement Moore's "A Visit from St. Nicholas."*

dinary booties and socks borrowed for holiday service. Homemakers might also decorate such stockings with embroidery or make more elaborate ones from cloth remnants. In the late 1800s, the first commercially made Christmas stockings became available. Most featured scenes printed on thin cotton or linen and were sold either already assembled or as patterns to be cut and sewn at home. The most popular images included Santa descending a brick chimney, an "x-ray" view of a stocking's contents, or scenes of stockings hung by the fire.

# Photography Credits

Cover, frontispiece, and pages 10-25, 28 (left), 32-35, 46-55, 62-68, 78, 88-97, 104-112, 120-121, 124-133: Steven Mays. Pages 8, 26-27, 28-31 (except 28 left), 36-45 (except 41 right and 45 right), 56-61 (except 56 left), 70-77, 80-85 (except 80 left), 114-119, 122-123, 134-167 (except 156-157 and 162-163): George Ross. Pages 41 (right), 45 (right), 80 (left), 162 (top left and bottom center), 163 (top row): Rob Whitcomb. Page 56 (left): Michael Luppino. Pages 86-87: (top row, left to right) The New York Public Library Picture Collection; courtesy of The Henry Francis duPont Winterthur Museum; The New York Public Library Picture Collection; Free Library of Philadelphia; (bottom row, left to right) The New York Public Library Picture Collection; Culver Pictures; Arizona Photographic Associates; The New York Public Library Picture Collection; Culver Pictures. Pages 98-103: David Lund, courtesy of *Houston Metropolitan Magazine*. Page 156 (far left): The Library of Congress.

# Prop Credits

The Editors would like to thank the following for their courtesy in lending items for photography. Items not listed below are privately owned. **Cover**: photographed at residence of Edwin Hild and Patrick Bell, Olde Hope Antiques, New Hope, PA; rocking chair, hooked rug, doll and chair, lantern, andirons—courtesy of Olde Hope Antiques; toy drummer, game board, large Steiff elephant pull toy, horn, heart motif doll cradle—collection of Mr. and Mrs. Anthony Lucera; doll bed and quilt, papier-mâché "spring lamb" candy container, small Steiff elephant pull toy, velvet chicken and duck pull toys, rocking-horse doll cradle—Jones Road Antiques, NYC; Santa Claus roly-poly—collection of Phillip Snyder, NYC; dried flowers on tree—Galerie Felix Flower, NYC; cookie cutter molds used for cookies—K. Dunwoody Tinsmith, Quarryville, PA; Christmas stockings—Jimmy Cramer, Keedysville, MD. **Page 8**: "Webster Farm" chair—Angel House, Brookfield, MA, chair fabric, "Raleigh Tavern" #178161, Williamsburg reproduction—Schumacher, NYC; preceding items, as well as other reproductions and antiques, available at Dilworthtown Country Store, West Chester, PA. **Pages 12-19**: antiques and contemporary folk art—American Country Antiques, Cedarburg, WI. **Page 14**: sheep pull toy in margin—Sandy Worrell (June Worrell Antiques), Houston, TX. **Pages 18-20**: photographed at American Country Farm, bed-and-breakfast guesthouse, Mequon, WI. **Pages 22-25**: wreaths designed by Richard Kollath, West Hurley, NY; Victorian-style paper gift tags—The Gifted Line, Sausalito, CA; hand-printed wallpaper, "Marigold," from *In the Morris Tradition*—Bradbury & Bradbury Art Wallpapers, Benicia, CA. **Pages 32-35**: gift wrappings created by Ginger Hansen Shafer, NYC; angel and Santa Claus stickers—The Gifted Line, Sausalito, CA. **Page 41**: candle bobs in margin—collection of Robert M. Merck, Weston, CT. **Page 45**: Santa Claus roly-poly in margin—collection of Phillip V. Snyder, NYC. **Pages 46-47**: paper gift tag—The Gifted Line, Sausalito, CA. **Page 48**: contemporary crafts on mantel—Christmas in the Country, at Cedar Creek Settlement, Cedarburg, WI; antiques—American Country Antiques, Cedarburg, WI. **Pages 49-53**: antiques—American Country Antiques, Cedarburg, WI; reproduction feather trees—Primitive Trees, Cedarburg, WI. **Page 56**: wallpaper and border—Bradbury & Bradbury Art Wallpapers, Benicia, CA. **Pages 58-59**: wallpaper border—Bradbury & Bradbury Art Wallpapers, Benicia, CA. **Pages 62-63**: cornucopias designed by Ginger Hansen Shafer, NYC; angel, Santa Claus, Christmas tree, heart stickers—The Gifted Line, Sausalito, CA. **Pages 64-66**: Santa Claus dolls—Susan Hale Studio, at Cedar Creek Settlement, Cedarburg, WI; reproduction feather trees—Primitive Trees, Cedarburg, WI; Christmas tins in margin—collection of Bonnie J. Slotnick, NYC. **Pages 70-71**: angel—Darla Karchella, Jersey Shore, PA; "Country Chippendale" sofa—Angel House, Brookfield, MA; sofa fabric, "Cranston Plaid" #645692—Waverly, NYC; "Tyler Lion" coverlet—Colonial Williamsburg reproduction; preceding items, as well as chandelier and other reproductions and antiques, available at the Dilworthtown Country Store, West Chester, PA. **Page 72**: angel—Darla Karchella, Jersey Shore, PA; curtain fabric, "Tavern Check" #81508, in document blue, a Williamsburg reproduction—Schumacher, NYC; "Essex Grist Mill" chair—Angel House, Brookfield, MA; homespun fabric on chair, "Plymouth" #81694, in oatmeal—Greeff, NYC; reproduction tavern table—Steven Dickerman, Lancaster, PA; preceding items, as well as tin candle sconce, available at Dilworthtown Country Store, West Chester, PA. **Pages 74-75**: rose hip wreath and other reproductions and antiques—Dilworthtown Country Store, West Chester, PA. **Pages 76-77**: reproduction three-tiered bobbin basket—Mailey's Pennsylvania Primitive, East Berlin, PA; log cabin—Dean Johnson, Keedysville, MD; preceding items, as well as antiques, available at the Dilworthtown Country Store, West Chester, PA. **Page 78**: chest and place mat—Origin, NYC; animal candleholders and green pottery pitcher—Amigo Country, NYC; terra-cotta crèche figures—Pan

American Phoenix, NYC. **Page 80**: Belsnickel cookie cutter in margin—collection of Mark Winchester, Annandale, VA. **Pages 96-97**: springerle cookies made by, and springerle molds from the collection of, William Woys Weaver, food historian, Devon, PA. **Pages 104-105**: garlands created by Ginger Hansen Shafer, NYC; glass fruit ornaments—Old World Christmas, Spokane, WA. **Pages 108-109**: pottery ornaments, teapot, bowls, cups—Rabbit Artworks, Santa Fe, NM; painted wooden iguana—Richard Davila, Santa Fe, NM; painted tin ornaments, toy trucks, tin toys, wooden circus—Jackalope, Santa Fe, NM. **Pages 110-111**: rabbit pottery—Rabbit Artworks, Santa Fe, NM; place mats, pepper wreaths, painted tin Christmas trees, terra-cotta figures—Jackalope, Santa Fe, NM; Christmas blocks and wooden sitting Santas—American Country Collection, Santa Fe, NM; wooden snake—Richard Davila, Santa Fe, NM; wooden rooster—Mark Kuick, Rio Rancho, NM. **Page 112**: blown-glass ornaments—Old World Christmas, Spokane, WA; dinner plates—Bill Goldsmith, available at Kitchen Classics, Bridgehampton, NY; brass candlestick and Regency chairs—J. Garvin Mecking, Inc., NYC; "Old Maryland Engraved" sterling silver flatware—Kirk Stieff Co., Baltimore, MD; wallcovering, "Townsend" #2590, in pearl, from *Winterthur,* vol. 1—Stroheim & Romann, Long Island City, NY; candle—Candlewick, Portland, MI. **Pages 116-117**: sgraffito plates—Dilworthtown Country Store, West Chester, PA. **Pages 120-121**: silver-plate Victorian breadbasket, Continental glass candlesticks—James II Galleries, NYC; "Ars Vivendi" bone china and "Torino" wine glasses—Villeroy & Boch, NYC; "Old Maryland Engraved" sterling silver flatware—Kirk Stieff Co., Baltimore, MD; "Orleans" linen tablecloth—Le Jacquard Français from Palais Royal, Charlottesville, VA; silver-plate candlesticks—Oneida Silversmiths, Oneida, NY; chairs—Pierre Deux Antiques, NYC; lace-trimmed napkins—Henri Bendel, NYC. **Pages 122-123**: wallpapers and borders—Bradbury & Bradbury Art Wallpapers, Benicia, CA. **Pages 124-125**: dinnerware—Spode, NYC. **Pages 128-129**: dinnerware—Rabbit Artworks, Santa Fe, NM; terra-cotta miniature pots and crèche figures—Jackalope, Santa Fe, NM; wooden snake—Richard Davila, Santa Fe, NM. **Pages 130-131**: table—Pierre Deux Antiques, NYC; small leaf tureen, "Salmon Fruit" serving bowl and dinner plates, round majolica platter with oysters, brass breadbasket, footed majolica compote with fruit, crystal decanter—Mottahedeh, NYC; ironstone platter with turkey, paisley shawl, antique Christmas ornaments, 19th-century redware crock with flowers, carving set, glass compote—Vito Giallo Antiques, NYC; brass candlesticks, ecru lace-trimmed napkin on table—Gear, NYC; "Diamant" oriental rug—ABC International Design Rugs, NYC. **Page 132**: napkins and tablecloth—Henri Bendel, NYC; "Enchantment" silver-plate flatware—Oneida Silversmiths, Oneida, NY. **Page 133**: napkins—Henri Bendel, NYC; dried-flower topiaries—Sura Kayla, NYC. **Pages 134, 150-151, 153, 161, 164-165**: Christmas collectibles—collection of Robert M. Merck, Weston, CT. **Pages 136-149, 152, 154-155, 158-159, 166-167**: Christmas collectibles—collections of Robert M. Merck, Weston, CT, and Phillip V. Snyder, NYC. **Pages 142-144**: wallcovering used in displays, "Townsend" #2590, in pearl, from *Winterthur,* vol. 1—Stroheim & Romann, Long Island City, NY. **Pages 152-153**: wallcovering, "Hadley" #2717, in hunter, from *Winterthur,* vol. 1—Stroheim & Romann, Long Island City, NY. **Pages 154-155**: wallcovering, "Shooting Stars" #2635, in indigo, from *Winterthur,* vol. 1—Stroheim & Romann, Long Island City, NY. **Page 160**: Christmas postcards—collections of Robert M. Merck, Weston, CT, Phillip V. Snyder, NYC, and Gotham Book Mart Gallery, NYC. **Pages 162-163**: Louis Prang Christmas cards—Top row: (except second from left) Malcolm Rogers, Riverhead, NY; (second from left) Hallmark Historical Collection, Hallmark Cards, Kansas City, MO. Bottom row: (except second from left) Hallmark Historical Collection, Hallmark Cards; (second from left) Malcolm Rogers.

# Index

# Acknowledgments

Our thanks to Patrick Bell, Robert and Cristina Davila Brodsky, Abbie Chaykin, Lee Cochran, Jimmy Cramer, Bobbie and Player Crosby, Weldine and John Dossett, Jane and Jack Fitzpatrick, Vito Giallo, Gotham Book Mart Gallery, Susan and Jack Hale, Hallmark Cards, Edwin Hild, Audrey and Doug Julian, Christina and Michael Kearney, Robert M. Merck, Bettie and Seymour Mintz, Judith and Dave Murtagh, Sandra and James Pape, Malcolm Rogers, Cynthia Schaffner, Phillip V. Snyder, Donna and Peter Steffen, Ed Weaver, William Woys Weaver, Ethel and Win Wilson, and Mark Winchester for their help on this book.

Second printing
Published simultaneously in Canada
School and library distribution by Silver Burdett Company,
Morristown, New Jersey

TIME-LIFE is a trademark of Time Incorporated U.S.A.

Production by Giga Communications, Inc.
Printed in U.S.A.

Library of Congress Cataloging-in-Publication Data

A Country Christmas.
p.  cm. — (American country)
ISBN 0-8094-6779-8. — ISBN 0-8094-6780-1 (lib. bdg.)
1. Christmas decorations—United States. 2. Christmas cookery.
I. Time-Life Books.   II. Series.
TT900.C4C675  1989
745.594'12—dc20   89-5194
CIP

*American Country* was created by Rebus, Inc., and published by Time-Life Books.

## REBUS, INC.

Publisher: RODNEY FRIEDMAN • Editor: MARYA DALRYMPLE
Executive Editor: RACHEL D. CARLEY • Managing Editor: BRENDA SAVARD • Consulting Editor: CHARLES L. MEE, JR.
Senior Editor: SUSAN B. GOODMAN • Copy Editor: ALEXA RIPLEY BARRE
Writers: JUDITH CRESSY, ROSEMARY G. RENNICKE • Freelance Writer: CAROL SPIER
Design Editors: NANCY MERNIT, CATHRYN SCHWING
Test Kitchen Director: GRACE YOUNG • Editor, The Country Letter: BONNIE J. SLOTNICK
Editorial Assistant: LEE CUTRONE • Contributing Editor: ANNE MOFFAT
Indexer: MARILYN FLAIG

Art Director: JUDITH HENRY • Associate Art Director: SARA REYNOLDS
Designers: AMY BERNIKER, TIMOTHY JEFFS
Photographer: STEVEN MAYS • Photo Editor: SUE ISRAEL
Photo Assistant: ROB WHITCOMB • Freelance Photographers: MICHAEL LUPPINO, GEORGE ROSS

Special Consultants for this book: ROBERT M. MERCK, PHILLIP V. SNYDER
Series Consultants: BOB CAHN, HELAINE W. FENDELMAN, LINDA C. FRANKLIN, GLORIA GALE,
KATHLEEN EAGEN JOHNSON, JUNE SPRIGG, CLAIRE WHITCOMB

Time-Life Books Inc. is a wholly owned subsidiary of TIME INCORPORATED.

Editor-in-Chief: JASON McMANUS • Chairman and Chief Executive Officer: J. RICHARD MUNRO
President and Chief Operating Officer: N. J. NICHOLAS JR. • Editorial Director: RICHARD B. STOLLEY

## THE TIME INC. BOOK COMPANY

President and Chief Executive Officer: KELSO F. SUTTON
President, Time Inc. Books Direct: CHRISTOPHER T. LINEN

## TIME-LIFE BOOKS INC.

Editor: GEORGE CONSTABLE • Executive Editor: ELLEN PHILLIPS
Director of Design: LOUIS KLEIN • Director of Editorial Resources: PHYLLIS K. WISE
Editorial Board: RUSSELL B. ADAMS JR., DALE M. BROWN, ROBERTA CONLAN, THOMAS H. FLAHERTY,
LEE HASSIG, JIM HICKS, DONIA ANN STEELE, ROSALIND STUBENBERG
Director of Photography and Research: JOHN CONRAD WEISER

President: JOHN M. FAHEY JR.
Senior Vice Presidents: ROBERT M. DeSENA, JAMES L. MERCER, PAUL R. STEWART, JOSEPH J. WARD
Vice Presidents: STEPHEN L. BAIR, STEPHEN L. GOLDSTEIN, JUANITA T. JAMES,
ANDREW P. KAPLAN, CAROL KAPLAN, SUSAN J. MARUYAMA, ROBERT H. SMITH
Supervisor of Quality Control: JAMES KING
Publisher: JOSEPH J. WARD

*For information about any Time-Life book please call 1-800-621-7026, or write:*
*Reader Information, Time-Life Customer Service*
*P.O. Box C-32068, Richmond, Virginia 23261-2068*

*Time-Life Books Inc. offers a wide range of fine recordings, including a Rock 'n' Roll Era series.*
*For subscription information, call 1-800-621-7026, or write TIME-LIFE MUSIC,*
*P.O. Box C-32068, Richmond, Virginia 23261-2068.*